*Stewart E. Cooper, PhD, ABPP*
*Editor*

# Evidence-Based Psychotherapy Practice in College Mental Health

*Evidence-Based Psychotherapy Practice in College Mental Health* has been co-published simultaneously as *Journal of College Student Psychotherapy*, Volume 20, Number 1 2005.

*Pre-publication REVIEWS, COMMENTARIES, EVALUATIONS . . .*

"This long-awaited review of evidenced-based therapeutic practices will be OF SIGNIFICANT VALUE TO UNIVERSITY COUNSELING AND MENTAL HEALTH CENTERS as they consider ways of enhancing therapeutic practice. It BRINGS TOGETHER SOME OF THE VERY BEST COUNSELING CENTER PRACTITIONERS AND MANAGERS TO ADDRESS THE MOST COMMON PRESENTING CONCERNS OF STUDENT CLIENTS. As we gather more 'evidence' on evidence-based psychotherapy, this book serves as an important, groundbreaking effort by highlighting the potential value of these forms of treatment for serving our student constituencies."

**Dennis Heitzmann, PhD**
*Director*
*Center for Counseling and Psychological Services*
*Penn State University*

The Haworth Press, Inc.

# Evidence-Based Psychotherapy Practice in College Mental Health

*Evidence-Based Psychotherapy Practice in College Mental Health* has been co-published simultaneously as *Journal of College Student Psychotherapy*, Volume 20, Number 1 2005.

# Monographic Separates from the *Journal of College Student Psychotherapy*™

For additional information on these and other Haworth Press titles, including descriptions, tables of contents, reviews, and prices, use the QuickSearch catalog at http://www.HaworthPress.com.

*Evidence-Based Psychotherapy in College Mental Health,* edited by Stewart E. Cooper, PhD (Vol. 20, No. 1, 2005). *An overview of the key issues concerning the use of evidence-based psychotherapy practice by college counseling centers.*

*Case Book of Brief Psychotherapy with College Students,* edited by Stewart E. Cooper, PhD, ABPP, James Archer, Jr., PhD, ABPP, and Leighton C. Whitaker, PhD, ABPP (Vol. 16, No. 1/2, 2001 and 3/4, 2002). *"Impressive. . . . A fascinating group of case studies. effectively demonstrates how time-sensitive therapy can be successfully integrated with a developmental approach. An excellent addition to the library of all clinicians working with college-aged clients and an ideal text." (Bob McGrath, PsyD, ABPP, Director, Counseling and Consultation Services, University of Wisconsin, Madison)*

*Helping Students Adapt to Graduate School: Making the Grade,* by Committee on the College Student, Group for the Advancement of Psychiatry (Vol. 14, No. 2, 1999). *"Breaks new ground by giving professors and students a guide to the graduate school experience. . . . Thoughtful and clear in both description and prescription; it will benefit both students and their advisors. . . . This is a very readable and helpful resource." (Robert M. Randolph, PhD, Senior Associate Dean, Office of the Dean of Students and Undergraduate Education, Massachusetts Institute of Technology, Cambridge, Massachusetts)*

*Campus Violence: Kinds, Causes, and Cures,* edited by Leighton C. Whitaker, PhD, and Jeffrey W. Pollard, PhD (Vol. 8, No. 1/2/3, 1994). *"An indispensable reference work for health educators, administrators, and mental health professionals." (Journal of American College Health)*

*College Student Development,* edited by Leighton C. Whitaker, PhD, and Richard E. Slimak, PhD (Vol. 6, No. 3/4, 1993). *"Provides college counselors and therapists with some of the most important developmental perspectives needed in today's work with students." (Educational Book Review)*

*College Student Suicide,* edited by Leighton C. Whitaker, PhD, and Richard E. Slimak, PhD (Vol. 4, No. 3/4, 1990). *"Belongs in the hands and minds of everyone who works with suicidal students in post-secondary education. . . . Would also be a good text for graduate courses in counseling, social work, psychology, or student services." (Suicide Information & Education Center (SIEC) Current Awareness Bulletin)*

*The Bulimic College Student: Evaluation, Treatment, and Prevention,* edited by Leighton C. Whitaker, PhD, and William N. Davis, PhD (Vol. 3, No. 2/3/4, 1989). *"An excellent tool for college mental health professionals . . . Practical information and guidelines are provided to help college personnel develop programs for the prevention and treatment of bulimia." (Journal of Nutritional Education)*

*Alcoholism/Chemical Dependency and the College Student,* edited by Timothy M. Rivinus, MD (Vol. 2, No. 3/4, 1988). *"This volume is a compilation of articles on several dimensions of the campus substance abuse problems. . . . A must for the clinician's and the administrator's reading list." (Michael Liepman, MD, Providence VA Medical Center, Rhode Island)*

*Parental Concerns in College Student Mental Health,* edited by Leighton C. Whitaker, PhD (Vol. 2, No. 1/2, 1988). *"A useful reference for parents and professionals concerning the everyday, yet hardly routine, psychological issues of the college student." (American Journal of Psychotherapy)*

# Evidence-Based Psychotherapy Practice in College Mental Health

Stewart E. Cooper, PhD, ABPP
Editor

*Evidence-Based Psychotherapy Practice in College Mental Health* has been co-published simultaneously as *Journal of College Student Psychotherapy*, Volume 20, Number 1 2005.

The Haworth Press, Inc.

New York • London • Victoria (AU)
**www.HaworthPress.com**

*Evidence-Based Psychotherapy Practice in College Mental Health* has been co-published simultaneously as *Journal of College Student Psychotherapy*, Volume 20, Number 1 2005.

The development, preparation, and publication of this work has been undertaken with great care. However, the publisher, employees, editors, and agents of The Haworth Press and all imprints of The Haworth Press, Inc., including The Haworth Medical Press® and Pharmaceutical Products Press®, are not responsible for any errors contained herein or for consequences that may ensue from use of materials or information contained in this work. Opinions expressed by the author(s) are not necessarily those of The Haworth Press, Inc. With regard to case studies, identities and circumstances of individuals discussed herein have been changed to protect confidentiality. Any resemblance to actual persons, living or dead, is entirely coincidental.

Cover design by Jennifer M. Gaska

**Library of Congress Cataloging-in-Publication Data**

Evidence-based psychotherapy practice in college mental health/Stewart E. Cooper, editor.
     p. cm.
     "Co-published simultaneously as Journal of College Student Psychotherapy, Volume 20, Number 1 2005."
     Includes bibliographical references and index.
     ISBN-13: 978-0-7890-3068-9 (hard cover : alk. paper)
     ISBN-10: 0-7890-3068-3 (hard cover : alk. paper)
     ISBN-13: 978-0-7890-3069-6 (soft cover : alk. paper)
     ISBN-10: 0-7890-3069-1 (soft cover : alk. paper)
     1. College students–Mental health services. 2. College students–Counseling of. 3. Evidence-based psychiatry. I. Cooper, Stewart Edwin, 1953-
  RC451.4.S7E75 2006
  616.89–dc22
                                              2005025130

# Indexing, Abstracting & Website/Internet Coverage

This section provides you with a list of major indexing & abstracting services and other tools for bibliographic access. That is to say, each service began covering this periodical during the year noted in the right column. Most Websites which are listed below have indicated that they will either post, disseminate, compile, archive, cite or alert their own Website users with research-based content from this work. (This list is as current as the copyright date of this publication.)

Abstracting, Website/Indexing Coverage ......... Year When Coverage Began

- *Applied Social Sciences Index & Abstracts (ASSIA)*
  *(Online: ASSI via Data-Star) (CDRom: ASSIA Plus)*
  *<http://www.csa.com>* ................................ 1987

- *Business Source Corporate: coverage of nearly 3,350 quality*
  *magazines and journals; designed to meet the diverse*
  *information needs of corporations; EBSCO Publishing*
  *<http://www.epnet.com/corporate/bsourcecorp.asp>* ......... 2001

- *Contents Pages in Education* ............................. 1987

- *EBSCOhost Electronic Journals Service (EJS)*
  *<http://ejournals.ebsco.com>* ........................... 2004

- *Educational Administration Abstracts (EAA)* ............... 1991

- *Educational Research Abstracts (ERA) (online database)*
  *<http://www.tandf.co.uk/era>* ........................... 2001

- *e-psyche, LLC <http://www.e-psyche.net>* ................. 2001

- *Family & Society Studies Worldwide <http://www.nisc.com>* .... 1986

- *Family Index Database <http://www.familyscholar.com>* ....... 2004

- *Google <http://www.google.com>* .......................... 2004

- *Google Scholar <http://scholar.google.com>* ............... 2004

- *Haworth Document Delivery Center*
  *<http://www.HaworthPress.com/journals/dds.asp>* .......... 1986

(continued)

- *Higher Education Abstracts, providing the latest in research & theory in more than 140 major topics* ................... 1987
- *International Bulletin of Bibliography on Education* .......... 1992
- *Links@Ovid (via CrossRef targeted DOI links) <http://www.ovid.com>.* ................................ 2005
- *MLA Intl Bibliography provides a classified listing & subject index for books & articles published on modern languages, literatures, folklore, & linguistics. Available in print and in several electronic versions. Indexes over 50,000 publications <http://www.mla.org>.* .................................. 2001
- *OCLC ArticleFirst <http://www.oclc.org/services/databases/>* .... 2002
- *OCLC ContentsFirst <http://www.oclc.org/services/databases/>* .. 2002
- *Ovid Linksolver (OpenURL link resolver via CrossRef targeted DOI links) <http://www.linksolver.com>.* ................. 2005
- *Psychological Abstracts (PsycINFO) <http://www.apa.org>* ..... 1987
- *Social Services Abstracts <http://www.csa.com>* .............. 1990
- *Social Work Abstracts <http://www.silverplatter.com/catalog/swab.htm>* ........... 1987
- *Sociological Abstracts (SA) <http://www.csa.com>* ............. 1990
- *Special Educational Needs Abstracts* ....................... 1989
- *zetoc <http://zetoc.mimas.ac.uk/>* .......................... 2004

*Special Bibliographic Notes related to special journal issues (separates) and indexing/abstracting:*

- indexing/abstracting services in this list will also cover material in any "separate" that is co-published simultaneously with Haworth's special thematic journal issue or DocuSerial. Indexing/abstracting usually covers material at the article/chapter level.
- monographic co-editions are intended for either non-subscribers or libraries which intend to purchase a second copy for their circulating collections.
- monographic co-editions are reported to all jobbers/wholesalers/approval plans. The source journal is listed as the "series" to assist the prevention of duplicate purchasing in the same manner utilized for books-in-series.
- to facilitate user/access services all indexing/abstracting services are encouraged to utilize the co-indexing entry note indicated at the bottom of the first page of each article/chapter/contribution.
- this is intended to assist a library user of any reference tool (whether print, electronic, online, or CD-ROM) to locate the monographic version if the library has purchased this version but not a subscription to the source journal.
- individual articles/chapters in any Haworth publication are also available through the Haworth Document Delivery Service (HDDS).

# Evidence-Based Psychotherapy Practice in College Mental Health

## CONTENTS

About the Contributors     xi

Preface     xiii

Chapter 1. Evidence-Based Psychotherapy Practice
in College Mental Health     1
*Stewart E. Cooper*

Chapter 2. Evidence-Based and Empirically Supported College
Counseling Center Treatment of Alcohol Related Issues     7
*Ian T. Birky*

Chapter 3. Evidenced-Based Treatment of Depression
in the College Population     23
*Carolyn L. Lee*

Chapter 4. Evidenced-Based Practice for Anxiety Disorders
in College Mental Health     33
*Thomas Baez*

Chapter 5. Evidence-Based Practice for Treatment
of Eating Disorders     49
*Jaquelyn Liss Resnick*

Chapter 6. Supervising Counseling Center Trainees in the Era
of Evidence-Based Practice     67
*Jesse Owen*
*Karen W. Tao*
*Emil R. Rodolfa*

Chapter 7. Evidence-Based Psychotherapy in College Mental
Health: Common Concerns and Implications for Practice
and Research     79
*Stewart E. Cooper*

Index     89

# ABOUT THE EDITOR

**Stewart E. Cooper, PhD, ABPP,** Counseling/Research Methodology, Indiana University, has served as Director of the Counseling Services for the past seventeen years and is Professor of Psychology at Valparaiso University. He earned his BA in psychology and his MS in counseling at Indiana University. Before joining the staff at Valparaiso University, he was a staff psychologist at the University of Missouri at Rolla. He holds a Diplomate in Counseling Psychology from the American Board of Professional Psychology (ABPP) and is a Fellow of Divisions 17 (Counseling) and 13 (Consulting Psychology) of the American Psychological Association.

His research has focused on the application of multivariate perspectives and methods to diverse counseling-psychology topics. He has published more than 60 articles, book chapters, and monographs on prevention, psychometric analysis, substance abuse, dual-career issues, organizational consultation, and sex therapy. Most of his scholarship has been on the college population and their mental health issues. He is co-author with Jim Archer of *Counseling and Mental Health Services on Campus: A Handbook of Contemporary Practices* (1998) and co-author along with Jim Archer and Leighton Whitaker of a *Case Book of Brief Psychotherapy with College Students* (2002). He currently serves as Associate Editor for the *Consulting Psychology Journal* and has served on the editorial boards for the *Journal of American College Health and Psychology Bulletin* and now for the *Journal of College Student Psychotherapy.*

Dr. Cooper has been active with the governing boards of the Association of University and College Counseling Center Directors (AUCCCD) and of the International Association of Counseling Services (IACS). He has also held a number of positions on the boards of Divisions 17 and 13 of the American Psychological Association. His current professional roles include clinical work, supervision, outreach and consultation, administration, teaching, and research.

# About the Contributors

**Thomas Baez** (PhD, Michigan State University) is a Senior Psychologist and Coordinator of Alcohol Services at the Counseling and Psychological Services Center of the University of Michigan in Ann Arbor, Michigan. He is Adjunct Assistant Professor at Michigan State University. His current research and practice interests focus on the treatment of anxiety disorders and public speaking phobias, bilingual counseling (English-Spanish), substance abuse, training and supervision, and group psychotherapy. In working with college students, Thomas combines cognitive behavioral, interpersonal psychotherapy and psychodrama based therapeutic approaches.

**Ian T. Birky** (PhD, Oklahoma State University) is Director of Counseling and Psychological Services at Lehigh University. He also teaches as an Associate Professor in the College of Education and the College of Arts and Sciences, Psychology Department. He was one of the principal investigators on a Robert Wood Johnson Foundation funded five year alcohol project and the primary investigator on a federally funded Department of Education grant supporting further alcohol research with collegiate varsity athletes. An avid runner, biker, swimmer and squash/tennis player, he serves in the capacity of sport psychologist for many of the varsity sport teams at Lehigh University and is a regular consultant to the athletic department.

**Carolyn L. Lee** (PhD, Indiana University) is Chief Psychologist at Indiana University Counseling and Psychological Services. She is a Diplomate of ABPP. She held faculty positions at Indiana State University and Hanover College. She has practiced privately, as well as worked in community mental health. She was trained in the use of Interpersonal Psychotherapy of Depression at Western Psychiatric Institutes and Clinics, Pittsburgh, Pennsylvania. She established and directed a Depression Treatment Clinic within a community mental health center utilizing that model. Her professional interests include depression treatment, anxiety and stress management, and depression prevention.

**Jesse Owen** (MEd) is a doctoral candidate in counseling psychology at the University of Denver. He received his Master's from the University of Miami, Florida and has also worked as a part-time professor at Metropolitan State College of Denver. Currently, he is a pre-doctoral intern at the University of California, Davis where he specializes in professional training and supervision. His other professional interests include diversity and mental health, couples therapy and research, epistemology, and clinical judgment strategies.

**Jaquelyn Liss Resnick** (PhD, University of Florida) is Director of the Counseling Center and Affiliate Professor in the departments of Psychology and Counselor Education at the University of Florida. She is current President of the Association of University and College Counseling Center Directors. She also is Vice President for Professional Practice for the Society of Counseling Psychology, Division 17 of the American Psychological Association (APA). She has served as President of the International Association of Counseling Services, Inc. Within APA, as well as other professional organizations, she has chaired committees on the status of women. For over 30 years, she has been an author, program presenter, workshop leader and consultant on various topics, including college student mental health, issues in counseling women, and advocacy.

**Emil R. Rodolfa** (PhD, Texas A&M University) is the Director of the University of California, Davis Counseling and Psychological Services (CAPS). He is chair of the Council of Chairs of Training Councils (CCTC), a member-at-large of the Board of Directors of the Association of State and Provincial Psychology Boards (ASPPB), past-chair of the Association of Psychology Postdoctoral and Internship Centers (APPIC) Board of Directors and is a former president of the California State Board of Psychology. His current research interests include supervision, ethical and legal issues, boundary dilemmas, and sequence of training issues.

**Karen W. Tao** (MA) is a psychology intern at the University of California, Davis Counseling and Psychological Services (CAPS) and a doctoral candidate at the University of Wisconsin-Madison in the Department of Counseling Psychology. Her research interests include multicultural competence in counseling, teaching and supervision, experiences of racial/ethnic minorities in higher education, and cultural factors in psychotherapy.

# Preface

This special volume is designed to provide some answers for the field of college student psychotherapy in relation to evidenced-based treatment (EBT). Our Editor, Stewart Cooper, PhD, ABPP and all of the authors have taken into account the considerable contrast between theory, research and practice in this field and the inherent assumptions of EBT. We intend that the answers will help college and university psychotherapists and counselors gain useful perspectives on how to respond to the rapidly increasing EBT movement.

Contrasting the conditions of college practice versus EBT research reveals many sharp differences that, in several instances, can appear ironic. For example, EBT commonly defines brief psychotherapy as 20 regularly scheduled consecutive sessions whereas most institutions of higher education average three or four sessions and have a modal sessions' number of one. Even in the relatively rare instances when there are more sessions per given student, the psychotherapy is likely to be discontinuous. Yet, EBT may be presented as geared economically to brief interventions where resources are quite limited. For these several other reasons the college therapist may feel that EBT is an impractical undertaking when practiced according to the current laboratory models.

The authors of this collection, however, did not merely dismiss the pursuit of EBT. They suggest ways of trying to do research and training that can assist rigor in practice without destroying EBT's credibility and relevance. They show that the simple adoption of the status quo in EBT research for use in college psychotherapy has quite lim-

[Haworth indexing entry note]: "Preface." Whitaker, Leighton C. Co-published simultaneously in *Journal of College Student Psychotherapy* (The Haworth Press, Inc.) Vol. 20, No. 1, 2005, pp. xvii-xviii; and: *Evidence-Based Psychotherapy Practice in College Mental Health* (ed: Stewart E. Cooper) The Haworth Press, Inc., 2005, pp. xiii-xiv. Single or multiple copies of this article are available for a fee from The Haworth Document Delivery Service [1-800-HAWORTH, 9:00 a.m. - 5:00 p.m. (EST). E-mail address: docdelivery@haworthpress.com].

*xiii*

ited usefulness. Thus, college psychotherapists are needed to inform research with their special knowledge and experience while their knowing about the EBT literature and how science can be related to the art of effective psychotherapy, can enhance their practice.

*Leighton C. Whitaker, PhD, ABPP*
*Editor, Journal of College Student Psychotherapy*

# Chapter 1.
# Evidence-Based Psychotherapy Practice in College Mental Health

Stewart E. Cooper

**SUMMARY.** This lead off article to the special volume on evidence-based psychotherapy (EBP) in college and university counseling and mental health centers presents an overview of the topic and outlines the structure of this publication. A focus on EBP research and practice generally, and in institutions of higher education specifically, is provided for depression, anxiety, eating, and alcohol use disorders, as well as a special chapter on training in EBP through college and university-based practicum and internship programs. The special volume ends with a chapter summarizing common concerns and issues identified about the applicability of EBPs to college mental health and presents recommendations for current and future evidence-based practice and research in college counseling center contexts. *[Article copies available for a fee from The Haworth Document Delivery Service: 1-800-HAWORTH. E-mail address: <docdelivery@haworthpress.com> Website: <http://www.HaworthPress.com> © 2005 by The Haworth Press, Inc. All rights reserved.]*

**KEYWORDS.** Evidence-based practice, college mental health, college counseling centers

Stewart E. Cooper, PhD, ABPP, is Director of Counseling Services and Professor of Psychology at Valparaiso University, 826 La Porte Avenue, Valparaiso, IN 46383.

Address correspondence to: Stewart Cooper (E-mail: stewart.cooper@valpo.edu).

[Haworth co-indexing entry note]: "Chapter 1. Evidence-Based Psychotherapy Practice in College Mental Health." Cooper, Stewart E. Co-published simultaneously in *Journal of College Student Psychotherapy* (The Haworth Press, Inc.) Vol. 20, No. 1, 2005, pp. 1-6; and: *Evidence-Based Psychotherapy Practice in College Mental Health* (ed: Stewart E. Cooper) The Haworth Press, Inc., 2005, pp. 1-6. Single or multiple copies of this article are available for a fee from The Haworth Document Delivery Service [1-800-HAWORTH, 9:00 a.m. - 5:00 p.m. (EST). E-mail address: docdelivery@haworthpress.com].

## INTRODUCTION TO THE SPECIAL PUBLICATION ON EVIDENCE-BASED PSYCHOTHERAPY IN COLLEGE MENTAL HEALTH

A zeitgeist is emerging surrounding the issue of evidence-based mental health counseling practice including that offered in college counseling centers. Indications of this movement can be found in multiple locations throughout professional psychiatry and psychology. For example, the American Psychiatric Association has invested significant resources in the development of practice guidelines for a variety of psychiatric disorders. These practice guidelines, which are available at *www.psych.org/psych_pract/treatg/pg/prac_guide.cfm*, comprise three components: a summary of recommendations for assessment, treatment, and special problems; an in-depth review of the literature; and directions for future research. Similarly, the Clinical Psychology Division of the American Psychological Association has published a list of more than 71 well-established or probably effective treatments for particular clinical syndromes, provided at *www.apa.org/about/division/div12.html*. Terms used in this emerging dialogue include empirically-validated treatment (EVT), empirically-based treatments (EBT), empirically-supported interventions (ESI), evidence-based practice (EBP), evidence-informed practice (EIP), and evidence-informed interventions (EII). Evidence-based practice (EBP) is employed as a more general term today and refers to all the above.

Over the past several years, Barlow (2000), Chambless and Hollon (1998), and Nathan and Gorman (2002) have each offered major contributions toward identifying empirically-validated treatments for specific disorders. The latter was unique in its incorporation of both medication and psychotherapeutic treatments. The hoped-for product would appear to be an elucidation of the most effective treatment methods to treat the major psychiatric illnesses *independent of factors about the client and the therapist*. An insightful and creative treatment of the empirically supported therapies topic was a trio of articles published by David Glenn and in the *Chronicle of Higher Education* (CHE, 2004, October 24). The first, *Nightmare Scenarios*, highlighted the twin errors of either ignoring scientific evidence in selecting and implementing treatment interventions or of buying into an overly narrow quantitatively rigorous standard for demonstrating research support. The second, *Sandplay, Therapy and Yoga*, described one professional organization's struggle to decide what material is or is not recognized as credible for CE credits. The third, *The Debriefing Debate*, presented how evidence on a particular intervention, in this case Critical Incidents Stress Debriefing, often shows contradictory findings.

Not all have agreed with this focus on a direct and limited association of specific interventions for particular disorders, however. A competing perspective, and one that a growing number of psychologists are advocating, is a focus on investigating the influences of the therapeutic relationship and other common influences on therapeutic outcomes. "It has been shown that evidence-based movements (a) overemphasize treatments and treatment differences, (b) ignore aspects of psychotherapy that have been shown to be related to outcome, such as variation among psychologists, the relationship, and other common factors" (Wampold & Bhati, 2004, p. 563). A synthesis of recent studies suggests that as much as twice of the variance of therapeutic outcome is accounted for by therapist/client factors as by specific treatments for particular syndromes. Consequently, Norcross (2001, 2002) and Wampold, Lichtenberg, and Waehler (2002) have championed this alternative emphasis on therapist/client factors. Of interest is that even a greater proportion of the variance of outcomes of therapy may be accounted for by client factors alone (Hanna, 2003).

As a consequence of these new perspectives, both Chalwisz (2003) and Wampold (2003) have argued that therapists who want to implement best practice should employ a balance of both qualitative and quantitative sources of information on outcomes in order to inform their selection of interventions. The journal, *Professional Psychology: Research and Practice*, recently included a special section that focused on evidence-based practice in psychology (Levant, Benedict, & Sammons, 2004). All four articles in this special section echoed the idea of an expanded view of what consists of credible "evidence." For example, Messer (2004) wrote: "Optimally, practitioners need to follow a model of evidence-based psychotherapy practice, such as the disciplined inquiry or local clinical scientist model, that encompasses a theoretical formulation, empirically supported treatments (ESTs), empirically supported therapy relationships, clinician's accumulated practical experience, and their clinical judgment about the case at hand." Edwards, Danillo, and Bromley (2004) argue that "important evidence about best practice comes from case-based research, which builds knowledge in a clinically useful manner and complements what is achieved by multivariate research methods" (p. 589).

A recent newsletter article from the Division of Counseling Psychology of APA adds a helpful longitudinal perspective. "In the last decade, a concerted effort has been made to evaluate the effectiveness of mental and behavioral health interventions. These efforts have included developing criteria and identifying empirically supported treatments, identifying empirically supported therapy relationships, disseminating criteria for evaluating treatment guidelines, and identifying principles evaluating evidence related to psychological interventions. These initiatives, to varying degrees, have influenced accreditation criteria, funding priorities, and the management and payment of services. Unfortunately, they have also created disagreement about the relative merits of identifying treatments and about how evidence should be used and interpreted relative to practice" (April 2004 SCP Newsletter, p. 15).

College counseling centers are being impacted by all the factors mentioned in the above paragraph. Specifically, staff therapists working in college mental health services are under significant press to deliver counseling services effectively and efficiently with several forces coming together to create this pressure. The level of resources available for higher education is under one of the largest challenges in its history, and non-academic costs, such as the provision of counseling services, are often vulnerable to cuts or elimination. Yet this stringency comes at a time of increasingly high demand for college counseling services for a population with increasingly severe psychopathology (though not all professionals agree with the latter). Simultaneously, the movement to show increased documentation of positive results has become pervasive. Most universities are under significant accreditation duress to have elaborated assessment and evaluation plans in place and to produce data showing positive outcomes, all of which takes more time and resources.

That campus-based mental health services counselors would "base" their practice on the available "scientific" evidence would seem almost a given. However, there are several significant problems that college counseling center therapists may have with evidence-based practice, especially how it has evolved thus far with the almost exclusive emphasis on empirically supported interventions and a very strong bias against more clinical forms of research. The first problem is that the majority of studies that have served as the basis for EBT define short-term therapy as 20 or even more sessions per "treatment episode." In college contexts, very time limited/very brief therapy models are the norm with a national average of only 3.3 sessions per client (Draper, Jennings, Baron, Erdur, & Shankar, 2002). A second problem, one that goes along time lines as well, is that the investigations employed for empirical validated counseling follow clients receiving an intact period of treatment. Yet university life, and therefore counseling, is often greatly affected by the academic calendar. Therapy often stops abruptly with academic breaks such as the end of fall, spring, or summer terms, or graduation. A third major problem is that virtually all the evidence-based studies use strict exclusion criteria eliminating all those with co-morbid diagnoses. In college contexts, clients with multiple issues are the norm, particularly among those presenting with more distressed symptoms, and clients having a diagnosis limited to one and only one major psychological problem are an exception. Yet a fourth significant confound is that evidence-based approaches are standardized and therapists using them must carefully follow structured treatment protocols. Adherence to these protocols is to be carefully monitored. Most practitioners in college mental health utilize integrative or eclectic approaches and many alter their practice with particular clients in line with the new multicultural counseling guidelines. A fifth problem, one already mentioned in this introduction, is the over-reliance on empirical forms of evidence as being the only legitimate forms of evidence. Case studies, single-subject designs, and intense study of a clinical issue or population represent more natural fits to the ongoing counseling process engaged in by often over-taxed counseling center staff.

The purpose of this special collection is to present the pros and cons of a focus on evidence-based practice in college mental health with four presenting problems very common to this population. Ian T. Birky of Lehigh University discusses Substance Abuse Disorders. Carolyn L. Lee, Indiana University, focuses on treatment of Depression. Thomas Baez, University of Michigan, covers Anxiety Disorders. Jaquelyn Liss Resnick, University of Florida, presents on Eating Disorders. Each of these four authors has been asked to address three questions. First, what are the "evidence-based" methods currently used for clinical assessment and treatment in this area, including any research that has been conducted in college settings recently? Second, how do the previously mentioned evidence-based approaches apply to the very brief/intermittent therapy that is practiced on most campuses? Third, what are the implications for practice and research for therapy as conducted in university mental health settings?

Next is on Supervising in the Era of Evidence-Based Practice by Jesse Owen, Karen Tao, and Emil Rodolfa of the University of California, Davis. They focus on facilitating the applied learning of EBP through campus-based training programs for practicum and intern students.

In the final chapter, I have noted the common concerns and issues articulated by the various contributing authors and made recommendations regarding evidence-based practice and research for those working in college counseling centers.

# REFERENCES

American Psychological Association (2001). Empirically supported therapy relationships: Conclusions and recommendations of the Division 29 Task Force. Psychotherapy: Theory, research, practice, training, 38, 495-497.

Barlow, D. H. (2000). Evidence-based practice: A world view. *Clinical Psychology: Science and Practice, 7,* 241-242.

Chalwisz, K. (2003). Evidence-based practice. *The Counseling Psychologist, 5,* 497-528.

Chambless, D.L., & Hollon, S.D. (1998). Defining empirically supported therapies. *Journal of Consulting and Clinical Psychology, 64,* 497-504.

Draper, M. R., Jennings, J., Baron, A., Erdur, O., & Shankar, L. (2002). Time-limited counseling outcome in a nationwide college counseling center sample. *Journal of College Counseling, 3,* 26-38.

Edwards, D. J., Dattilio, F. M., & Bromley, D. B. (2004). Developing evidence-based practice: The role of case-based research. *Professional Psychology: Research and Practice, 35,* 589-597.

Glenn, D. (2003, Oct. 24). Nightmare scenarios. *The Chronicle of Higher Education.*

Glenn, D. (2003, Oct. 24). Sandplay, therapy and yoga: Do they belong in continuing-education courses for psychologists? *The Chronicle of Higher Education.*

Glenn, D. (2003, Oct. 24). The debriefing debate: One popular therapy is called into question. *The Chronicle of Higher Education.*

Hanna, F. J. (2004). *Therapy with difficult clients: Using the precursors model to awaken change.* Washington, DC: APA Press.

Messer, S. B. (2004). Evidence-based practice: Beyond empirically supported treatments. *Professional Psychology: Research and Practice, 35,* 580-588.

Nathan, P. E., & Gorman, J. M. (2002). *A guide to treatments that work (2nd ed.).* New York: Oxford University Press.

Norcross, J. C. (Ed.). (2002). *Psychotherapy relationships that work: Therapist contributions and their responsiveness to patient needs.* New York: Oxford University Press.

Wampold, B. E., & Bhati, K. S. (2004). Attending to the omissions: A historical examination of evidence-based practice movements. *Professional Psychology: Research and Practice, 35,* 563-570.

# Chapter 2.
# Evidence-Based and Empirically Supported College Counseling Center Treatment of Alcohol Related Issues

## Ian T. Birky

**SUMMARY.** College counseling center administrators and staff counselors face the increasing challenge to provide best practice counseling in all domains of their work. The present chapter explores the evidence base for alcohol counseling, seeking to determine whether recent empirical evidence suggests the use of particular counseling strategies when working with alcohol related issues. A summary of research findings in general as well as specific to college counseling centers is provided, along with factors to consider when deciding how to best use the current evidence. *[Article copies available for a fee from The Haworth Document Delivery Service: 1-800-HAWORTH. E-mail address: <docdelivery@haworthpress.com> Website: <http://www.HaworthPress.com> © 2005 by The Haworth Press, Inc. All rights reserved.]*

**KEYWORDS.** Evidence-based, empirical support, counseling center, alcohol treatment

Ian T. Birky, PhD, is Director of University Counseling and Psychological Services and Associate Professor, Lehigh University, 36 University Drive, Bethlehem, PA 18015-3060 (E-mail: itb0@lehigh.edu).

[Haworth co-indexing entry note]: "Chapter 2. Evidence-Based and Empirically Supported College Counseling Center Treatment of Alcohol Related Issues" Birky, Ian T. Co-published simultaneously in *Journal of College Student Psychotherapy* (The Haworth Press, Inc.) Vol. 20, No. 1, 2005, pp. 7-21; and: *Evidence-Based Psychotherapy Practice in College Mental Health* (ed: Stewart E. Cooper) The Haworth Press, Inc., 2005, pp. 7-21. Single or multiple copies of this article are available for a fee from The Haworth Document Delivery Service [1-800-HAWORTH, 9:00 a.m. - 5:00 p.m. (EST). E-mail address: docdelivery@haworthpress.com].

Available online at http://www.haworthpress.com/web/JCSP
doi:10.1300/J035v20n01_02

During the past two decades, university and college counseling center staff occasionally attempted to prove, sometimes with the support of the Fund for the Improvement of Postsecondary Education (FIPSE) and Department of Education (DOE) federal grants, that the right combination of creative strategizing, hard work, persistence and money could produce intervention programs capable of significantly diminishing the amount of alcohol consumed on college campuses as well as decrease drinking related problems. Alcohol services and programs were designed in accordance with grant-inspired promises, offices were built, staff members were hired, and administrative oversight was designed to address this challenge. Despite FIPSE and DOE guidelines discouraging reliance on "therapy" as the cure agent for the "alcohol problem," some programmatic strategies explicitly contained "counseling" as one mechanism for change. This insistence on a "therapy" component was not surprising given that counselors and psychotherapists sometimes were members of the FIPSE teams. It was also evident that some of these counselors were unwilling to rely solely on ubiquitous information and education programs to alter drinking behavior in significant and lasting ways among college students, and defended counseling as a viable process for change.

Partly as a result of expectations linked to those grants, as well as broader challenges inspired by increasing institutional requirements for accountability in numerous university administrative domains, a growing challenge gradually developed to show that counseling-based alcohol interventions worked. Concurrently, there have been increasing efforts to determine whether there is evidential or empirical support for psychotherapeutic interventions. Evaluation of counseling center based treatments for problems related to alcohol have not escaped this scrutiny. Thus, the moment is right to evaluate the extent to which a credible evidence base exists for counseling center based alcohol treatments, and more broadly to consider if an evidence-based approach is a valuable and appropriate perspective from which to consider the alcohol-related work in college counseling centers. In order to maintain focus on the treatment issues in this chapter, the language used to reference therapists or counselors working in university or college mental health based counseling centers providing counseling or psychotherapy will simply make use of the words counseling and counseling center staff.

This chapter provides an overview of studies designed to evaluate the evidential base for alcohol treatments provided by counseling center staff. Also, it covers issues involved in conceptualizing the problem of how to evaluate studies designed to answer questions related to empirically based evidence for alcohol treatment in counseling centers. Finally, the chapter concludes with a number of comments regarding the feasibility and limitations of adhering to evidence-based treatment approaches when making decisions about alcohol-focused psychotherapy delivered within counseling centers, and provides brief suggestions for one conceptual framework with promise for informing contemporary treatment.

## *OVERVIEW*

At the outset, questions are raised in this chapter as to whether counselors or clinical administrators are in a position to promote and offer alcohol treatment therapies and protocols based on results arising from research evidence or other empirically based criteria. In an effort to answer these questions, some writers have recommended that counselors and researchers use broad-based determinants of evidence-based practice rather than simply those informed by positivistic, empirically based findings (Chwalisz, 2003). It is likely that this suggestion arises because to date, published survey and meta-analytic studies reporting on the success of specifically instituted therapies, and on therapies to address actual drinking-associated behaviors have found very limited evidence for claims of success (Werch, Pappas, & Castellon-Vogel, 1996; Nelson & Wechsler, 2001; Walters & Bennett, 2000). With regard to the alcohol treatment focus, these conclusions stand despite a vast but somewhat diffuse literature with purported claims that particular programs at specific universities with particular target audiences have been shown to significantly change the identified behaviors or conditions. A number of individual studies might convey such success, but Chambless and Hollon (1998) remind us that a careful analysis of the evidence suggests that treatment success most likely occurred on a particular campus because of factors specific to that college or university, the informed and participating personnel working there, and the specifically targeted and selected clientele solicited by the researchers. They also point out that far too few authors provided any significant real-world evidence of meaningful change and most were remiss in providing clear directions allowing for replication of their methodologies. In conclusion, they note that when the combined results of singular efforts to show treatment success were analyzed with meta-analytic methods and Bayesian approaches to hypothesis testing, there was little if any empirical evidence of success (Chambless & Hollon, 1998).

## REVIEW OF EXISTING RESEARCH
## AND CONCEPTUAL FRAMEWORK

Despite initial indications that the bar may be set too high if we demand practice policies formulated primarily from empirically based guidelines, a brief review of related literature may help us draw better conclusions regarding administrative and clinical decisions about treatment and competency guidelines for counselors addressing alcohol issues with college students. Before limiting our inquiry to counseling center based empirically tested interventions, it may be important for counselors to acknowledge the benefit of first determining whether there is empirical or evidence-based support for claims of alcohol counseling success in any setting (Wampold, Lichtenberg, & Waehler, 2002).

In looking at the research available, there does appear to be some evidence that specifically designed alcohol treatments "work." Using the current prescriptive descriptions and relatively strict criteria of Chwalisz (2003) who promoted evidence-based exploration using a range of empirical, clinical summation and even single case studies, counselors will note that supportive-expressive therapy and cognitive therapy "hold promise" for treating alcohol problems (Chambless et al., 1998). So, too, do behavioral therapy and interventions providing reinforcement for abstinence (Project Match Research Group, 1997). According to a meta-analysis by DeRubeis and Crits-Christoph (1997) and the Project Match Research Group (1997, 1998) and in line with the level of certainty criteria proffered by Wampold et al. (2002), there also seems to be "some possible" evidential support for efficacious treatments using social skills training (Monti, Kadden, Rohsenow, Cooney, & Abrams, 2002), cue exposure (Dawe, Rees, Mattick, Sitharthan, & Heather, 2002; Sitharthan, Sitharthan, Hough, & Kavanagh, 1997), "urge coping skills training" (Palfai, Monti, Colby, & Rohsenow, 1997), cognitive behavioral coping skills therapy (Kadden, Cooney, Getter, Litt, 1989; O'Leary & Monti, 2002), motivational enhancement therapy (Kahler et al., 2004), and 12-Step facilitation therapies (Tonigan, Toscova, & Miller, 1996). However, in making these statements, the evaluators of these meta-based studies equivocate in their support of the findings. They do so because they were frequently limited in their efforts to draw substantive conclusions by the necessity of reliance on research with questionable designs, poor generalizability, and difficult to replicate methodologies.

Given efforts to look specifically for evidence of effective therapy-based alcohol interventions derived from studies conducted on college campuses and specific to college counseling centers, counselors are quickly confronted with the paucity of applicable research. To attempt to complete their survey by utilizing evidence of "interventions" that work, Walters and Bennett (2000) point out that this effort is actually complicated by the fact that much of the literature is based on primary prevention work. Their review of the empirical support for this primary prevention work may be very helpful for counseling staff developing and delivering outreach programs, but they note that very little applicable research has been conducted assessing secondary or tertiary intervention outcomes. To select an alcohol treatment based on the results of primary alcohol prevention work on college campuses is equivalent to selecting one's therapy approach for depression based on studies of counseling center staff conducting depression and suicide programs in the residence halls. Nevertheless, published literature addressing this question includes a number of claims for success utilizing brief alcohol related treatments.

Using the criteria of Chambless and Hollon (1998), who suggest that counseling decisions are best informed by empirically based findings, it is clear that there are few studies with strong evidence for claims of success in decreased drinking or drinking related problems among college students following counseling interventions. Nevertheless, there have been efforts to explore these questions. One study using a single-session intervention comprised of education and assessment of current usage in reference to peers reported results of decreased drinking and fewer negative consequences from drinking during the next four years of college (Marlatt et al., 1998; Baer, Kivlahan, Blume, McKnight, Marlatt, 2001). It should be noted, however, that the students treated were not drawn from the pool of regular counseling-center clientele, but rather were first-year students identified as heavy drinkers, selected by the university to undergo the single session counseling intervention. Using a similar brief, single counseling session intervention that provided feedback regarding personal consumption in relation to peer drinking norms, as well as education about alcohol-related problems, researchers found some support for claims of decreased drinking, although without coincident or significant drinking related problem reduction (Borsari & Carey, 2000).

With the exception of this research, counselors looking for guidance in treating students seeking assistance for alcohol-related problems are left with little supporting empirical evidence to guide their work. Even for counseling center staff doing outreach programs, except for the quasi-experimental findings of health advocates such as Haines and Spear (1996) or Berkowitz and Perkins (1986) who have championed personalized and social norm educational strategies, stand-alone information-based educational methods show little promise for the everyday work of counseling centers. Personalized feedback, attitudinal change techniques, and skills-based approaches, however, show some promise for reducing alcohol problems, at least in the short term (Walters & Bennett, 2000).

Referenced in the previously identified counseling center based research was mention of brief or single-session interventions. In keeping with the trend toward brief treatment in counseling centers, alcohol research in the past decade has focused on brief individual therapy or brief individual interventions using personalized and social norm comparison feedback, motivational interviewing, education and behavioral monitoring (Borsari & Carey, 2000; Larimer et al., 2001; Roberts, Kivlahan, Baer, Neal, & Marlatt, 2000; Walters, Bennett, & Miller, 2000). There is some evidence that brief treatment for alcohol-related issues is equal to or more effective than long-term treatment, especially with self-referred clients (Bien, Miller, & Tonigan, 1993; Dimeff, Baer, Kivlahan, & Marlatt, 1999). These researchers also found that increasing treatment dosage does not correlate with similar increases in treatment gains. Although not supported by large amounts of evidence, brief treatments look fairly promising for alcohol counseling.

In sum, while there is no clear and strong evidence supporting a clinical agenda for persuading counseling center staff to begin using specific approaches to alcohol counseling, on the face of it, the number and variety of treatments purporting to demonstrate some individual counseling effectiveness is remarkable. Unless counselors remain wary, quantity rather than quality of research findings might influence treatment norms and create standards for practice. Because of this, counselors might attempt to convince themselves that professional integrity and open-mindedness require utilization of the "most promising" of the treatments studied, although this limitation hardly seems defensible without concurrently engaging in serious discussion about what to do with the numerous contrary claims and limited evidence. Awareness of the limitations of evidence-based practice in the treatment of college students with alcohol problems would be a helpful addition to that discussion.

# LIMITATIONS OF THE EVIDENCE-BASED APPROACH TO COLLEGE COUNSELING SERVICES

Counselors, before agreeing to practice a specific alcohol treatment, might justifiably ask the following questions to determine whether the approach selected was based on replicable alcohol treatment-based studies: (1) Do the research participants upon whom the reported conclusions were based match the real-life students attending sessions in the counseling center? Many studies were conducted on voluntary participants unlike the preponderance of center clients mandated or referred for treatment by judicially minded deans. Moreover, some of the research participants were paid or otherwise rewarded for participation and some had symptom profiles (i.e., selected because of self reported binge drinking in high school) typically very different from the students with whom center staff engage and are familiar with in the counseling center (i.e., referred by a third party for drinking offenses (Sadler & Scott, 1993)). (2) What outcome measures were used and are they meaningful to the treatment mandate or goals agreed upon in the typical college setting? Published results were often based on outcome measures such as decreased stress levels, increased employment reliability, establishment of alternate recreational activities, and score changes on assessment instruments attuned to attitude and knowledge rather than to specifically measured behavior critical to thriving in college (Chambless & Hollon, 1998). Other conclusions were based on findings that brief therapy worked at least as well as long-term inpatient treatment. Such comparisons between clients of inpatient treatment and college students seeing counselors for underage drinking offenses hardly seem beneficial or relevant.

Other questions could include: (3) What differential-change factors or outcome measures were studied in the published research? Researchers sometimes assessed reported alcohol intake, levels of anxiety, social ease, and interpersonal involvement without necessarily evaluating measurable indices of property damage, social disruption, financial costs, and loss of productivity. Conclusions about real-world change become suspect given the infrequency of substantive long-term effects, evidence of high drop-out rates, and researcher selection of change factors other than abstinence or closely related secondary effects such as property damage that are typically of most concern to university administrators. Finally, (4) Are the investigations replicable and are the promoted therapies teachable to clinical staff? In all cases, the use of replicable manualized intervention formats and randomized clinical trials were in short supply or absent.

It would seem that the careful and perhaps cautious reader of the literature would likely conclude that research evidence in this clinical area is often dependent on short-term laboratory interventions of questionable ecological validity and weak (even though statistically significant) empirical support. Actually, then, since findings from the research are equivocal at best, clinical practice influenced by this research is primarily based on gradual theoretically developed professional consensus. While such a professional consensus might be based on well meaning efforts to seek guidance from empirical research, at this point in time it is as likely that the "common factors" of effective counselor delivery may account for much of the reported change. Given that "common factors" such as a good therapeutic relationship account for some treatment induced change under almost any circumstance, at the present time there may be little advantage to claiming intervention selection guidance from the questionably relevant alcohol treatment studies. In attempting to make a decision whether to practice any particular treatment strategy, counselors left with some ambivalence might do well to appeal to the counseling profession's own standards for guidance.

## RECOMMENDED APPROACH FOR COLLEGE COUNSELORS

College-based counseling is generally recognized as a specialty clinical practice, and efforts are made constantly to provide services within the context of best practice standards that are guided by applicable research and wisdom gleaned from the totality of a long history of professional consensus acquired via research, case conferences and clinical experience. For various reasons, some of which will be addressed in the following, research in the area of alcohol counseling is still in its infancy (New STG on Evidence-Based Practice, 2004), presently offering only general constructs that counselors can try to integrate into clinical practice strongly influenced by our knowledge of common-factor elements for successful counseling. Lest counseling center staff, facing challenges to "make a difference" when treating the seemingly intractable problems of alcohol use on college campuses, feel inclined to maintain strict adherence to empirically based guidelines for providing "alcohol oriented treatment," it becomes important to recognize the following limitations in taking such an approach.

First, empirically defined treatment is or might best be based on a clearly defined diagnostic criterion for treatment and perhaps DSM-IV criteria could be used for comparison purposes. However, because DSM-IV diagnoses of alcohol pathology or associated problems may be unhelpful and thus are frequently not used in working with the majority of college students (Winters, 2001), there does not appear to be a universal standard for comparison across subject populations at the present time. Perhaps because of difficulty obtaining adequate numbers of participants, counseling center-based research typically has not included those clients with alcohol dependence or diagnosed abusive drinking, but rather the traditional heavy-using high school graduate perceived to be at risk because of patterns of prior use. These voluntary research participants, given brief treatment interventions in an educational format, provide questionable comparisons to most college students who involuntarily attend counseling sessions because of a single episode of alcohol misuse. Finally, while some students do attend because of personal concerns about possible addiction, loss of control, or because of needing to manage significant consequences of drinking, studies in college counseling centers have not focused on this population.

Second, in the university setting, most students are referred to alcohol-related services in the counseling center because of legally defined underage drinking offenses rather than because of diagnosed psychopathology. Those coerced into contact for reasons other than underage drinking are typically mandated because of some behavioral indiscretion of which alcohol was assumed to have been the causal culprit. In either case, center administrators set policy about treating judicially mandated clients and center staff members are then faced with confirming attendance, or if providing further services, deciding whether the diagnostic assessment and invitation-to-treatment focus is on the behavior (i.e., violence, injury, property damage) or the alcohol use itself (i.e., amount, frequency, illegality). Little if any research has provided findings leading to recommendations regarding conceptualizing work with the alcohol mandated client or pertaining to operational definitions of successful treatment. For judicially referred alcohol misuse cases, treatment success might administratively be best defined as completing the paperwork notifying the referring dean that the student fulfilled the required visit to the counseling center. Treatment success might also be indicated by effective use of the time spent introducing the student to the full range of psychotherapeutic services, inviting future use of the services if needed, or providing support for ongoing contact with a parole officer, a dean, or perhaps the parents.

Third, few if any helpful guidelines regarding how and under what circumstances referrals should be made following assessment and how decisions might be informed by diagnostic considerations exist at the present time. Scholars have not addressed either the reality or effectiveness of counseling center interventions in which a student, because of behavioral infractions and diagnosed alcohol dependence, is given a referral to an outpatient alcohol specialist, to an outpatient programmed treatment setting, or back to the home environment. In such cases, center staff might be relieved to know that effective and best practice treatment may well be referral of such students elsewhere or to intensive drug treatment programs if they can be clearly identified with DSM-IV descriptors for abuse or dependency.

Fourth, most clients attending sessions because of alcohol-related issues do not present voluntarily and most do not believe they have a problem. Few students have experienced significant long-term or frequently consistent evidence of negative consequences to believe they have a problem requiring assistance (Smith & Anderson, 2001). Even if they have such a history, most are, at best, in the contemplative stage of problem acknowledgement and have little intent to set goals for change (Prochaska, DiClementi, & Norcross, 1992). Because clients with alcohol issues seldom present voluntarily on that account, research methodologies should take into consideration the possible and probable differences between these clients and those students with depression or anxiety who frequently self-refer for treatment (Westen & Morrison, 2001). Researchers and counselors would do well to ask whether the probability of any subsequent attendance is related to experiences during the mandated session, and which interventions or therapist characteristics prompt client compliance to invitations for continuing sessions. Many college counselors choose simply to assess, recommend, and offer invitations to engage in therapy rather than assume ongoing responsibility for mandated clients. A common-factors perspective may be critical for understanding which counselor variables such as attitude and style seem to be critical for most beneficially taking advantage of the brief window of opportunity for intervention (Miller, Kilmer, Kim, Weingardt, & Marlatt, 2001; Rollnick & Miller, 1995).

Fifth, perhaps more so than with other students, clients with alcohol issues typically present with problems diagnostically co-morbid with and influenced by a variety of other factors (Clark, Wood, & Cornelius, 2003). Alcohol co-morbid with depression may look different than when co-morbid with anxiety, character disorder diagnoses, poly-drug use, attention deficit disorders, or learning disabilities. Additionally, it is reasonable for counselors to question whether and how treatment effectiveness varies with multicultural demographic variables such as academic status, social class, or with race and ethnicity. Gender and religious orientation may also correlate with treatment response and utilization. Especially with college students struggling with chemical substances, it is presumptuous for counselors to assume that it is helpful to discuss treatment efficacy related to some uni-dimensional factor such as amount or frequency of alcohol used.

## CONCLUSION

Perhaps it is not surprising to discover that little consensus has formed in support of specific evidence-based treatment efficacy with respect to the treatment of alcohol abuse or dependence. As the very recent Division 17 Special Task Group (New STG on evidence-based practice, 2004) realized and announced, selection of empirically based treatments for some presenting problems is functionally at a developmental stage whereby counselors are left to struggle with identification and conceptualization of the topical area itself. Further work is needed before we can determine how to bring the collaborative pieces together and recommend various models and strategies for research and practice. Elements for study necessarily include those of diagnostic problem assessment and identification, empirical and (or versus) qualitative results, co-morbidity with other diagnostic variables, influence of multicultural variables, treatment type or therapy orientation, referral factors, and other outcome variables.

In an effort to decide how to practice alcohol-related work while further evidence accumulates, counselors would do well to focus primarily on templates that can provide helpful heuristic and practical frameworks to assist their work with students struggling with alcohol related issues. Models created by such frameworks would allow counselors to address the treatment focus and effect as well as the amount of treatment provided. Using patient response-focused and dosage-effect models whereby the number of session contacts and measured gains are accounted for, college counselors may more successfully address matters of legitimate real-world intervention success in light of the number of sessions available for the intervention, the phase of treatment, and client commitment variables (Garfield, 1998).

As Chambless and Hollon (1998) point out, when counselors adopt such models, they can begin to determine the kinds of change and effect sizes reasonably expectable in a real-world population of college students given the use of brief intervention treatments. Using this type of approach, university-based counselors can learn to appreciate the effects they can procure during the college years, without assuming that their failure to show drinking related effects 5 or 10 years into the future means their interventions were ineffective or ill-advised. Thus, if counselors determine, based on dose-effect outcomes, that it would take more sessions to procure a desired response than counseling center resources allow, then determinations of success would need to be assessed from the vantage of a broader perspective.

Successful counseling might ultimately include recommendations for withdrawal from the university or referral to a treatment program that can provide the full dosage effect (Lambert, Hansen, & Finch, 2001). Research informed by such a framework might prompt replicable quantitative and qualitative methodologies relevant and applicable to the counseling center setting. Finally, practice within the frame of such models may allow counselors, relying on a very contemporary post-modern blend of quantitative and qualitative research results, the means to determine with their clients how best to discuss matters of subjective well-being, symptom reduction, and recovery of life functioning gains even if these matters are likely to be more seriously addressed in some future counseling work.

## REFERENCES

Baer, J. S., Kivlahan, D. R., Blume, A. W., McKnight, P., & Marlatt, G. A. (2001). Brief intervention for heavy-drinking college students: 4-year follow-up and natural history. *American Journal of Public Health, 91*, 1310-1316.

Berkowitz, A. D., & Perkins, H. W. (1986). Problem drinking among college students: A review of recent research. *Journal of American College Health, 35*, 21-28.

Bien, T. H., Miller, W. R., & Tonigan, J. S. (1993). Brief interventions for alcohol problems: A review. *Addiction, 88*, 315-335.

Borsari, B., & Carey, K. (2000). Effects of a brief motivational intervention with college student drinkers. *Journal of Consulting & Clinical Psychology, 68*, 728-733.

Chambless, D. L., Baker, M. J., Baucom, D. H., Beutler, L. E., Calhoun, K. S., Crits-Christoph, P. et al. (1998). Update on empirically validated therapies: II. *The Clinical Psychologist, 51*, 3-16.

Chambless, D. L., & Hollon, S. (1998). Defining empirically supported therapies. *Journal of Consulting & Clinical Psychology, 66*, 7-18.

Chwalisz, K. (2003). Evidence-based practice: A framework for twenty-first-century scientist-practitioner training. *The Counseling Psychologist, 5*, 497-528.

Clark, D. B., Wood, D. S., & Cornelius, J. R. (2003). Clinical practices in the pharmacological treatment of co-morbid psychopathology in adolescents with alcohol use disorders. *Journal of Substance Abuse Treatment, 25,* 293-295.

Dawe, S., Rees, V., Mattick, R., Sitharthan, T., & Heather, N. (2002). Efficacy of moderation-oriented cue exposure for problem drinkers: A randomized controlled trial. *Journal of Consulting & Clinical Psychology, 70,* 1045-1050.

DeRubeis, R. J., & Crits-Christoph, P. (1998). Empirically supported individual and group psychological treatments for adult mental disorders. *Journal of Consulting & Clinical Psychology, 66,* 37-52.

Dimeff, L. A., Baer, J. S., Kivlahan, D. R., & Marlatt, G. A. (1999). *Brief Alcohol Screening and Intervention for College Students (BASICS): A Harm Reduction Approach.* New York, NY: Guilford Press.

Garfield, S. (1998). Some comments of empirically supported treatments. *Journal of Consulting & Clinical Psychology, 66,* 121-125.

Haines, M., & Spear, S. (1996). Changing the perception of the norm: A strategy to decrease binge drinking among college students. *Journal of American College Health, 45,* 134-140.

Kadden, R. M., Cooney, N. L., Getter, H., & Litt, M. D. (1989). Matching alcoholics to coping skills or interactional therapies: Posttreatment results. *Journal of Consulting & Clinical Psychology, 57,* 698-704.

Kahler, C., Read, J., Ramsey, S., Stuart, G., McCrady, B., & Brown, R. (2004). Motivational Enhancement for 12-Step Involvement Among Patients Undergoing Alcohol Detoxification. *Journal of Consulting & Clinical Psychology, 72,* 736-741.

Lambert, M. J., Hansen, N. B., & Finch, A. E. (2001). Patient-focused research: Using patient outcome data to enhance treatment effects. *Journal of Consulting & Clinical Psychology, 69,* 159-172.

Larimer, M. E., Turner, A. P., Anderson, B. K., Fader, J. S., Kilmer, J. R., Palmer, R. S. et al. (2001). Evaluating a brief alcohol intervention with fraternities. *Journal of Studies on Alcohol, 62,* 370-380.

Marlatt, G., Baer, J., Kivlahan, D., Dimeff, L., Larimer, M., Quigley, L., Somers, J., & Williams, E. (1998). Screening and brief intervention for high-risk college student drinkers: From a two-year follow-up assessment. *Journal of Consulting & Clinical Psychology, 66,* 604-615.

Miller, E. T., Kilmer, J. R., Kim, E. L., Weingardt, K. R., & Marlatt, G. A. (2001). Alcohol skills training for college students. In P. M. Monti, S. M. Colby, & T. A. O'Leary (Eds.), *Adolescents, alcohol, and substance abuse: Reaching teens through brief interventions* (pp. 109-141). New York, NY: The Guilford Press.

Monti, P. M., Kadden, R. M., Rohsenow, D. J., Cooney, N. L., & Abrams, D. B. (2002). *Treating alcohol dependence: A coping skills training guide* (2nd ed.). New York, NY: The Guilford Press.

New STG (Special Task Group) on evidence-based practice. (2004, April). *Division 17 Newsletter, 25,* 15.

O'Leary, T. A., & Monti, P. M. (2002). Cognitive-behavioral therapy for alcohol addiction. In S. G. Hofmann & M. C. Tompson (Eds.), *Treating chronic and severe mental disorders: A handbook of empirically supported interventions* (pp. 234-257). New York, NY: The Guilford Press.

Palfai, T. P., Monti, P. M., Colby, S. M., & Rohsenow, D. J. (1997). Effects of suppressing the urge to drink on the accessibility of alcohol outcome expectancies. *Behaviour Research & Therapy, 35*, 59-65.

Prochaska, J. O., DiClementi, C. C., & Norcross, J. C. (1992). In search of how people change: Applications to addictive behavior. *American Psychologist, 47*, 1102-1114.

Project Match Research Group. (1997). Matching alcoholism treatments to client heterogeneity: Project Match post-treatment drinking outcomes. *Journal of Studies on Alcohol, 58*, 7-29.

Project Match Research Group. (1998). Matching alcoholism treatments to client heterogeneity: Project MATCH three-year drinking outcomes. *Alcoholism: Clinical & Experimental Research, 22*, 1300-1311.

Roberts, L. J., Kivlahan, D. R., Baer, J. S., Neal, D. J., & Marlatt, G. A. (2000). Individual drinking changes following a brief intervention among college students: Clinical significance in an indicated preventive context. *Journal of Consulting & Clinical Psychology, 68*, 500-505.

Rollnick, S., & Miller, W. R. (1995). What is motivational interviewing? *Behavioral and Cognitive Psychotherapy, 23*, 325-334.

Sadler, O. W., & Scott, A. M. (1993). First offenders: A systematic response to underage drinking on the college campus. *Journal of Alcohol and Drug Education, 38*, 62-71.

Sitharthan, T., Sitharthan, G., Hough, M. J., & Kavanagh, D. J. (1997). Cue exposure in moderation drinking: A comparison with cognitive-behavior therapy. *Journal of Consulting & Clinical Psychology, 65*, 878-882.

Smith, G. T., & Anderson, K. G. (2001). Personality and learning factors combine to create risk for adolescent problem drinking: A model and suggestions for intervention. In P. M. Monti, S. M. Colby, & T. A. O'Leary (Eds.), *Adolescents, alcohol, and substance abuse: Reaching teens through brief interventions* (pp. 109-141). New York, NY: The Guilford Press.

Tonigan, J. S., Toscova, R., & Miller, W. R. (1996). Meta-analysis of the literature on Alcoholics Anonymous: Sample and study characteristics moderate findings. *Journal of Studies on Alcohol, 57*, 65-72.

Walters, S. T., & Bennett, M. E. (2000). Addressing drinking among college students: A review of the empirical literature. *Alcoholism Treatment Quarterly, 18*, 61-77.

Walters, S. T., Bennett, M. E., & Miller, J. H. (2000). Reducing alcohol use in college students: A controlled trial of two brief interventions. *Journal of Drug Education, 30*, 361-372.

Wampold, B. E., Lichtenberg, J. W., & Waehler, C. A. (2002). Principles of empirically supported interventions in counseling psychology. *Counseling Psychologist, 30*, 197-217.

Werch, C. E., Pappas, D. M., & Castellon-Vogel, E. A. (1996). Drug use and prevention efforts at colleges and universities in the United States. *Substance Use & Misuse, 31*, 65-80.

Westen, D., & Morrison, K. (2001). A multidimensional meta-analysis of treatments for depression, panic, and generalized anxiety disorder: An empirical examination of the status of empirically supported therapies. *Journal of Consulting & Clinical Psychology, 69,* 875-899.

Winters, K. C. (2001). Assessing adolescent substance use problems and other areas of functioning. In P. M. Monti, S. M. Colby & T. A. O'Leary (Eds.), *Adolescents, Alcohol and Substance Abuse* (pp. 80-108). New York: The Guilford Press.

# Chapter 3.
# Evidenced-Based Treatment of Depression in the College Population

Carolyn L. Lee

**SUMMARY.** This review explores evidence-based treatment for depression within the college and university population. Treatments for depression in adults are among the most rigorous studied treatment modalities in the psychotherapy literature, providing consistent evidence for the efficacy of at least two treatments, cognitive behavioral therapy and interpersonal psychotherapy for depression, but the evidence for use of these therapies within the college population is sparse and inconclusive. The length of psychotherapy, diagnostic purity, and lack of adherence to specific theoretical models may be important elements contributing to the lack of treatment research on this population. More research should be focused on developing and evaluating specific treatments, which might address some of the unique stresses and dynamics within the college population. *[Article copies available for a fee from The Haworth Document Delivery Service: 1-800-HAWORTH. E-mail address: <docdelivery@haworthpress.com> Website: <http://www.HaworthPress.com> © 2005 by The Haworth Press, Inc. All rights reserved.]*

**KEYWORDS.** College students, psychotherapy, depression

Carolyn L. Lee, PhD, ABPP, is Chief Psychologist at Indiana University Counseling and Psychological Services, 600 North Jordan Avenue, Bloomington, IN 47405 (E-mail: cllee@indiana.edu).

[Haworth co-indexing entry note]: "Chapter 3. Evidenced-Based Treatment of Depression in the College Population." Lee, Carolyn L. Co-published simultaneously in *Journal of College Student Psychotherapy* (The Haworth Press, Inc.) Vol. 20, No. 1, 2005, pp. 23-31; and: *Evidence-Based Psychotherapy Practice in College Mental Health* (ed: Stewart E. Cooper) The Haworth Press, Inc., 2005, pp. 23-31. Single or multiple copies of this article are available for a fee from The Haworth Document Delivery Service [1-800-HAWORTH, 9:00 a.m. - 5:00 p.m. (EST). E-mail address: docdelivery@haworthpress.com].

Available online at http://www.haworthpress.com/web/JCSP
doi:10.1300/J035v20n01_03

Depressive disorders may be the most common psychological disorders experienced by college students. A survey of more than 47,000 students on 74 campuses in the spring of 2003 conducted by the American College Health Association reported that 18.9 percent of the students had experienced some symptoms of depression, though perhaps not the full symptom picture of a clinical depression. Voelker (2003) cites a utilization survey conducted at Kansas State University. That survey found that the number of students seeking services to alleviate depression in 1988-1992 compared with 1996-2001 rose from 21 to 41 percent. Voelker's (2003) article suggests that college counseling centers in most other institutions have experienced similar increases in utilization. Kadison and DiGeronimo (2004) echo these findings stating that the incidence of depression on college campuses has doubled in the past 15 years. The data from the American College Health Association shows a 4.6 percent increase in the incidence of depression among college students over the four years from 2000 to 2004. In those surveys 14.9 percent of students in the 2004 survey group reported a lifetime incidence of diagnosed depression, whereas only 10.3 percent of the 2000 survey group reported ever having been diagnosed with depression. Given these trends, it is extremely important to consider efficacious ways to treat depression among the college population.

The two most rigorously studied treatments for depression are cognitive behavioral therapy (Beck, Rush, Shaw, & Emory, 1979) and interpersonal therapy for depression (Klerman, Weissman, Rounsaville, & Chevron, 1984). Both the cognitive behavioral and interpersonal therapies have detailed manuals outlining the treatment, and both have been subjected to "clinical trials," similar in nature to medical drug trials, in which the researchers have attempted to control for so-called extraneous variables. "Purity" is sought with respect to diagnostic criteria used for selection of patients, therapist adherence to the therapy, and length of treatment.

Further, in "clinical psychotherapy trials" therapists are specifically trained in the particular model of treatment under evaluation, adherence to the prescribed treatment condition is deemed necessary for an adequate evaluation of the treatment modality, and patient outcomes are assessed systematically and uniformly. Moreover, patients are screened with respect to diagnostic criteria and are excluded if they do not meet all of the criteria for major depression (in fact, in many studies recurrent depressions must be evident). These research studies used criteria similar to the Diagnostic and Statistical Manual-III (1980) definition of depression which require patients to have depressed mood or loss of interest/pleasure towards most daily activities for at least two weeks, and a cluster of four of seven symptoms including changes in sleep and appetite, psychomotor agitation or retardation, fatigue, feelings of worthlessness or guilt, problems concentrating or making decisions, and thoughts of death or suicide (DSM-III, 1980). Patients are excluded when co-morbid conditions such as panic disorder, substance abuse disorders, and personality disorders (categories A and B) exist. Given the rigid exclusion criteria, a large number of potential clients are excluded from participation. The exclusion rates found in a recent meta-analysis of treatment of depression studies range from 42% to 86% (Weston & Morrison, 2001).

These clinical trial studies have been criticized as not representative of psychological treatment as it is usually practiced. For example, it is hard to imagine excluding 42 to 86 percent of depressed clients in the university counseling center setting because they have co-morbid diagnostic features. Additionally, finding ways to induce adherence to specific treatment modalities would be difficult in many college mental health settings where high proportions of the staff value integrative or eclectic counseling approaches. Though these studies have been criticized as being overly divorced from the "real world" practice of psychology, they remain prototypical of the empirical method to psychotherapy research. And when insurers and health care administrators talk about "empirically validated treatments for depression," these therapies (and various psychopharmacological interventions) and the body of literature surrounding them are generally what they have in mind.

If we were to simply ask the question–"Is there empirical evidence supporting the use of particular types of psychotherapy for the treatment of depression in the college or university setting?"–the answer would probably have to be "No." A few studies that attempt to test particular types of therapy such as cognitive behavioral or interpersonal (Hogg & Deffenbacker, 1988; Pace & Dixon, 1993) have been undertaken, but sustained and systematic efforts to conduct this type of investigation are lacking. The result is a few, very small "n" studies which may appear promising, but which are truly inconclusive about the efficacy of these treatments within the college population. Beyond the problem of small sample size, most of these studies lack sufficient rigor to allow clear demonstrations of the efficacy of the psychotherapies with this population. Additionally, the number of sessions in the typical study with college students is eight, whereas the number of sessions in the main "evidence-based research" investigations on similar psychotherapies that have received systematic study over the past couple of decades is 12 to 16.

On the other hand, these therapies as practiced in university mental health settings may bear enough similarity to those "evidence-based" psychotherapies evaluated with the general adult population (ages 18-60) that we can reasonably apply them to the college population. Or perhaps, we should say that given the lack of convincing evidence against their use, they are the best "evidence-based" treatments we have to offer at this time.

It should be noted, however, that there might also be reasons that cognitive-behavioral and interpersonal therapies might not be the best choices for the treatment of college students. Specifically, students may be particularly at risk for depression because of the lifestyle that seems inherent to the college experience, including adapting to a new environment, substance use, and chronic sleep deprivation (Voelker, 2004). In support of this, Furr, Westerfield, McConnell and Jenkins' (2001) survey of students at four different college and universities (1455 students in the combined sample) found that 53% had experienced what they would term depression since beginning college. The top four "causes" of their depression were grade problems, loneliness, money problems, and boyfriend/girlfriend relationship problems. Bonner and Rush (1988) suggest that the prevalence of depression among college samples is twice that of age-peers who are not in college. Thus, the collective stresses and experiences of college students may be unique to them, and treatments with utility for the general populations, even those including college-aged people, might not generalize well to college settings. At the present time, no research is available to answer this question.

## THE REAL MEANING OF BRIEF THERAPY IN COLLEGE POPULATIONS

Largely stemming from utilization/resources disparity, many university and college counseling centers have been put under pressure to utilize very short-term or brief treatment methods. This often translates into specific session limits or subtle pressure to be brief because of the continual influx of clients. Thus, one question is how the specific treatments advocated by the clinical trials research might translate into usage in the university setting.

It is difficult to do tightly-controlled research in the college population with "naturally occurring" clientele. Most clinical trials of psychotherapy have used some type of manual-driven, duration specific treatment in an effort to ensure consistency amongst clinicians providing the treatment. The prototype of this research is the NIMH Treatment of Depression Collaborative Research Project (Elkins, Shea, Watkins, Imber, Sotsky, Collins, Glass, Pilkonis, Leber, Dockerty, Fiester, & Parloff, 1989). This study examined the use of cognitive behavioral therapy (CBT), interpersonal psychotherapy for depression (IPT), and psychopharmacology, both alone and combined with the psychotherapies. The length of treatment in this study was 16 weeks. While there is some variation among studies, treatment episodes in the typical research design last from 12 or 16 weeks. The research designs required adherence to a particular treatment modality plus a minimum length of treatment to be sufficiently tested. A common outcome measure is the percent of "completers," i.e., those who improved under a specific treatment and time condition.

The number of sessions is of particular interest in this discussion of psychotherapy in the college counseling center setting. Draper, Jennings, Baron, Erdur, and Shankar (2002) provide information from surveying 42 member universities in the Research Consortium of Counseling and Psychological Services in Higher Education. These universities were mostly state-supported ranging in size from 2,000 to 48,000 students with most schools within the range of 15,000 to 25,000. They report on a pool of 4,679 clients who sought services during the 1997-1998 academic year. Thirty-four percent of clients either failed to return after intake or to respond to intake or the Outcome Questionnaire-45 (OQ45). Moreover, 1,336 students declined to follow through with the study or failed to complete sufficient questionnaire information. Thus, they end up reporting on only 1,761 participants or 38% of the potential client sample. In this subsample, the modal number of sessions was 1 and the average number of sessions 3.3 (SD 2.4). These facts begin to illuminate the difficulty of doing evidence-based psychotherapy research within the university setting with its "naturally-occurring" population. It seems that the typical college student client does not stay in therapy long enough to benefit from the types of evidence-based psychotherapies investigated in the literature.

Draper et al. (2002), in their introduction section, note that most of the counseling centers involved in their research employed a brief treatment model. They commented in their discussion section that since they did not have "session limits" (an assigned number of session), they had no groupings large enough (20 or more participants) for clients who attended more than 10 sessions to generate meaningful data, somehow implying that had they had a defined number of sessions that they could have enticed more students to stay in treatment. This may be so, although the attrition rates in most clinical trials, which explicitly specify the number of psychotherapy sessions, is also quite high (Westen et al., 2001). Moreover, it seems important to address the typical population of clients under study.

The data gathered to support evidence-based treatments is based on studies that specify a particular number of treatment sessions, usually between 8 and 16. Since most of the college students are not meeting those expectations, it is not clear that those treatment modalities would pertain to the "real world population." It seems little wonder that we lack anything approaching consistent "clinical trials" within the university setting.

However, on a more positive note, the Draper et al. (2002) report is consistent with the general psychotherapy literature documenting that psychotherapy, in general, is helpful in reducing psychological distress. No consistent theoretical orientation was specified or identified, yet improvement was noted across sessions within those university samples involved in that study. However, the percent "improved" is still modest at best, though the longer a student stayed in counseling, the more they seemed to improve, at least until the eighth to tenth sessions subsequent to which the increased magnitude of gain was quite small.

## WHAT'S A COLLEGE
## COUNSELING CENTER THERAPIST TO DO?

The American Psychological Association (2002) advanced three criteria for suggesting treatment guidelines: empirical research, clinical judgment and expertise, and acceptability to the patient. As suggested in the preceding discussion, the jury is still out as to whether the CBT and IPT therapies, that have demonstrated efficacy with respect to the treatment of depression in the general population, are applicable to the college setting. Further research is needed in that area. Moreover, the debate about specific treatments (i.e., CBT, and IPT) vs. common factors and empirically-supported (therapy) relationship factors is applicable to this discussion. Each "camp" seems to have support for their position. That is, there is support for the efficacy of specific treatments; there is support for common factors, and there is support for relationship factors (which may be a subcomponent of common factors). "Clinical judgment and expertise" is likely to vary from clinician to clinician depending on their training and experiences. The same is true for "acceptability to the patient" which will vary with the patient's previous experiences, worldview, and the ways in which treatment issues are presented to the client.

One possibility is that university-based clinicians can utilize the evidence-based treatments, if they have the training to do so, with selected sets of the college-aged population. For example, young people who are mourning the loss of a loved one might be motivated to stay in treatment longer than average (for college students seeking therapy). Those individuals might benefit from interpersonal psychotherapy for depression to address issues of grief, since grief is one of the specific problem foci of that treatment. In other instances, cognitive behavioral techniques might be very helpful for people with strong tendencies to engage in catastrophic thinking, especially about academic or relational matters.

It should be emphasized that common factors are at work in specific treatments, as well as nonspecific and/or untested interventions, and future research needs to find ways to both tease apart these dimensions and discover how they combine, and in what circumstance, for effective treatment (Chwalisz, 2001; Beutler, 2002). These common factors probably account for the improvement seen in the general psychotherapy literature where specific therapies are not manual-driven and tested. Special attention needs to be focused on the college populations. Although there is some research to suggest that the psychotherapeutic services provided by counseling centers are helpful to students (Draper et al., 2001), treatment approaches need to be elucidated and refined, especially in this day of increasing accountability. More research needs to be done to determine what short-term modalities will be most effective, in what time frame, and what will help students stay in treatment long enough to make significant clinical gains.

## DISCUSSION

Some of the best efficacy studies have been conducted on treatments for depression with the general adult population (ages 18 to 60), but few studies have been done specifically on the treatment of depression with the college counseling center population. However, the existing studies tend to support the broader findings that behavioral, cognitive behavioral and interpersonal treatments are viable, evidence-supported treatments for depression in the college-aged population. A significant problem in the "real world" of therapy in university settings may be to find ways of helping students remain in treatment long enough to benefit from them.

Alternately, it might be important to look at developing and evaluating short(er)-term therapies (perhaps six to eight sessions in length), specifically for the college-age population with complaints of major depression. It may be that given the multiple demands on their time combined with the additional affects on availability due to the academic schedule, we need to find ways to efficiently address their concerns by creating a "packaged" treatment of short duration that is more consistent with their naturally-occurring staying power in therapy. Moreover, the unique stresses of the college environment might need to be considered in creating treatments. For example, many students experience an exacerbation of depressive tendencies in the "heat" of academic pressures, and then experience a lessening of depressive symptoms once the "heat is turned down" between semesters or quarters. This type of dynamic is acknowledged clinically, but is seldom addressed in the treatment literature in any rigorous way. This "syndrome" may be quite different than clinical depressions among non-college populations.

There are more questions than answers with respect to treating college students who complain of depression. The pressures to use evidence-based treatments are likely to remain the zeitgeist in the foreseeable future. It may actually intensify as public scrutiny is high with respect to counseling service availability on college campuses. It may also be that the best defense is to develop and test treatments specifically designed for the college population, taking into account some of the unique stresses of that population.

## REFERENCES

American Psychiatric Association. (1980). *Diagnositic and statistical manual of mental disorders. (3rd ed.).* Washington, D.C: Author.

American Psychological Association. (2002). Criteria for evaluating treatment guidelines. *American Psychologist,* 57(12), 1052-1059.

Beck, A. T., Rush, A. J., Shaw, B. F., & Emery, G. (1979). *Cognitive Therapy of Depression.* New York: Guilford Press.

Beutler, L. J. (2002). The dodo bird is extinct. *Clinical psychology: Science and practice,* 9(1), 31-34.

Bonner, R. L., & Rush, A. R. (1988). A prospective investigation of suicidal ideation in college students: A test of a model. *Suicide and Life Threatening Behavior,* 18(3), 245-258.

Chwalisz, K. (2001). A common factors revolution: Let's not "cut off our discipline's nose to spite its face." *Journal of Counseling Psychology*, 48(3), 262-267.

Draper, M. R., Jennings, J., Baron, A., Erdur, O., & Shankar, L. (2002). Time-limited counseling outcome in a nationwide college counseling center sample. *Journal of College Counseling*, 3, 26-38.

Elkins, I., Shea, M. T., Watkins, J. T., Imber, S. D., Sotsky, S. M., Collins, J. F., Glass, D. R., Pilkonis, P. A., Leber, W. R., Dockerty, J. P., Fiester, S. J., & Parloff, M. B. (1989). NIMH treatment of depression Collaborative research program: General effectiveness of treatments. *Archives of General Psychiatry*, 46, 971-983

Furr, S. R., Westefeld, J. S., McConnell, G. N., & Jenkins, J. M. (1988). Suicide and depression among college students: A decade later. *Professional Psychology: Research and Practice*, 32(1), 97-100.

Hogg, J. A. & Deffenbacker, J. L. (1988). A comparison of cognitive and interpersonal-process group therapies in the treatment of depression among college students. *Journal of Counseling Psychology*, 35(3), 304-310.

Kadison, R. & DiGeronimo, T. F. (2004). *College of the overwhelmed: The campus mental health crisis and what to do about it.* New York: Jossey-Bass.

Klerman, G. L., Weissman, M. M., Rounsaville, B. J., & Chevron, E. S. (1984). *Interpersonal psychotherapy of depression.* New York: Basic Books.

National College Health Assessment (2000-2004). American College Health Association (www.acha.org).

Pace, T. M. & Dixon, D. N. (1993). Changes in depressive self-schemata and depressive symptoms following cognitive therapy. *Journal of Counseling Psychology*, 40(3), 288-294.

Voelker, R. (2003). Mounting student depression taxing campus mental health services. *Journal of the American Medical Association*, 289(16), 2055-2056.

Voelker, R. (2004) Stress, sleep loss, and substance abuse create potent recipe for college depression. *Journal of the American Medical Association*, 291(18), 2177-2179.

Weston, D. & Morrison, K. (2001). A multidimensional meta-analysis of treatments of depression, panic and generalized anxiety disorder: An empirical examination of the status of empirically supported therapies. *Journal of Consulting & Clinical Psychology*, 69(6), 875-899.

# Chapter 4.
# Evidenced-Based Practice
# for Anxiety Disorders in College Mental Health

## Thomas Baez

**SUMMARY.** Anxiety disorders are the most common mental health concerns in the United States and they tend to be among the most frequently reported in college mental health. While efficacious research for the psychotherapy treatment of specific anxiety disorders (e.g., social phobia, panic disorder, etc.) exists, the picture is more complex in clinical practice especially with students who are treated as a whole person, usually involving multiple co-existing disorders as well as normal developmental challenges of adjusting to college. This chapter reviews the evidenced-based research for anxiety disorders in both the general population and the college student population, as well as evidence for therapist/relationship factors. It examines the numerous challenges for conducting effectiveness studies in college mental health, suggestions for working with chronically anxious college students, and future directions for research and practice in this area. *[Article copies available for a fee from The Haworth Document Delivery Service: 1-800-HAWORTH. E-mail address: <docdelivery@haworthpress.com> Website: <http://www.HaworthPress.com> © 2005 by The Haworth Press, Inc. All rights reserved.]*

Thomas Baez, PhD, is a Senior Psychologist and coordinator for alcohol services at the Counseling and Psychological Services Center of the University of Michigan, 3100 Michigan Union, Ann Arbor, MI 48109 (E-mail: tbaez@umich.edu).

[Haworth co-indexing entry note]: "Chapter 4. Evidenced-Based Practice for Anxiety Disorders in College Mental Health" Baez, Thomas. Co-published simultaneously in *Journal of College Student Psychotherapy* (The Haworth Press, Inc.) Vol. 20, No. 1, 2005, pp. 33-48; and: *Evidence-Based Psychotherapy Practice in College Mental Health* (ed: Stewart E. Cooper) The Haworth Press, Inc., 2005, pp. 33-48. Single or multiple copies of this article are available for a fee from The Haworth Document Delivery Service [1-800-HAWORTH, 9:00 a.m. - 5:00 p.m. (EST). E-mail address: docdelivery@haworthpress.com].

Available online at http://www.haworthpress.com/web/JCSP
doi:10.1300/J035v20n01_04

**KEYWORDS.** Anxiety disorders, empirically supported treatments, evidenced-based treatments, college mental health, college students, effectiveness studies, efficacious studies, common factors, therapist/relationship factors

Given the incidence and prevalence of anxiety disorders among university students and the continuing likelihood of limited resources, therapists working in college counseling center contexts have many reasons to want to know about evidence-based practice (EBP). This chapter on anxiety disorders and treatment among college students by college mental health professionals addresses several aspects. First, the incidence, co-morbidity, and their impact on academic success and quality of life are covered. This is followed by a summary of evidenced-based treatments for anxiety disorders in the general population and in college mental health. Evidence for therapist/relationship factors in psychotherapy outcomes is then mentioned. The final sections of the work address challenges and suggestions for conducting EBP research and clinical practice with college students with anxiety problems. Future directions and questions for research and practice with anxiety disorders are also covered. Finally, a brief summary and conclusions are given.

## INCIDENCE, CO-MORBIDITY AND THEIR EFFECTS ON ACADEMIC SUCCESS AND QUALITY OF LIFE

Anxiety Disorders are the most common mental illnesses in the United States, affecting 19.1 million (13.3%) of the adult population between the ages of 18-54. (Anxiety Disorders Association of America, 2003). They may develop from a variety of risk factors including genetics, personality and life events. The anxiety disorders are grouped in six categories including: generalized anxiety disorders (GAD, 4 million), obsessive compulsive disorder (OCD, 3.3 million), panic disorder (PD, 2.4 million), posttraumatic stress disorder (PTSD, 5.2 million), social anxiety disorder (SAD, 5.3 million) and specific phobias (11.5 million). The economic impact of anxiety disorders on the U.S. economy is estimated at 42 billion a year, including 22.84 billion attributed to repeated use of healthcare facilities.

In examining clients presenting problems at counseling centers, Benton, Robertson, Tseng, Newton, and Benton (2003) found that anxiety concerns tend to be among the most frequently reported client problems. Specifically, in their 13-year span study, the rate of stress/anxiety increased a full 26% (from 36.26% in 1988 to 62.87% in 2001). Anxiety disorders often have a detrimental impact on students' academic performance, attendance, retention, career selection, relationship development, as well as on their physical health and general well being. The treatment of these disorders among college students is frequently complex and difficult because clinical levels of anxiety are associated with increased risk of depression, substance abuse, and suicidal thoughts (Olfson, Marcus, Wan, & Geissler, 2004). As counseling centers continue to move toward brief therapy models of practice and greater emphasis on addressing more immediate or situational concerns, severe anxiety problems accumulate, requiring more time and more profound change for which students seek counseling.

## EVIDENCED-BASED TREATMENTS (EBT) FOR ANXIETY DISORDERS IN THE GENERAL POPULATION

College counselors should first learn what is known about EBT with anxiety disorders in the general adult population. The majority of empirically supported treatments for the various anxiety disorders are concentrated on a variety of Cognitive Therapy and Behavior Therapy techniques (see Table 1). The investigations of these approaches have been judged as meeting the guidelines for Type I and II empirically supported treatments (Chambless, 2002; Chambless & Ollendick, 2001; Nathan & Gorman, 2002) which generally indicate clinical trials, manualized treatments, single diagnosis limitations, training and monitoring therapist adherence, managing the dose of intervention, random assignment to treatments, and blind evaluation procedures. The general anxiety disorder efficacy studies seem to support active treatments including Applied Relaxation, Cognitive Therapy and Cognitive Behavioral Therapy (CBT), whereas the obsessive compulsive disorder efficacy studies tend to support anxiety exposure followed by response prevention, and CBT. The panic disorder studies support in-vivo exposure, CBT, and applied relaxation, and the Post Traumatic Stress Disorder (PTSD) efficacy studies support exposure, stress inoculation, and the use of Eye Movement Desensitization and Reprocessing (EMDR), which also includes a desensitization component. Studies on the treatment of social anxiety/phobia efficacy indicate that social skills training procedures, relaxation training, exposure-based methods, CBT/group, and systematic desensitization are effective. With specific phobias,

TABLE 1. Evidenced-Based Supportive Interventions for Anxiety Disorders

| Anxiety Disorders Classification | Evidenced-Based Supportive Treatments |
|---|---|
| Generalized Anxiety Disorder | Active Treatments<br>Applied Relaxation<br>Cognitive Therapy/CBT |
| Obsessive Compulsive Disorder | Exposure<br>Response Prevention<br>CBT |
| Panic Disorder | Exposure (In Vivo)<br>CBT<br>Applied Relaxation |
| PTSD | Exposure<br>Stress Inoculation<br>EMDR |
| Social Anxiety/Phobia | Social Skills Training<br>Relaxation<br>Exposure-Based Methods<br>CBT/Group<br>Systematic Desensitization |
| Specific Phobias | In Vivo Exposure<br>CBT<br>Relaxation<br>Systematic Desensitization |

Summarized from: Chambless & Ollendick (2001) and Nathan & Gorman (2002).

in-vivo exposure procedures, CBT, relaxation, and systematic desensitization appear to work successfully.

Results of several meta-analytic studies on psychotherapy outcomes for anxiety disorders, which tend to be based on the above listed psychotherapy approaches, are promising. For example, in the treatment of agoraphobia, Andrews (1982) found an effect size (measures the strength of a relation) of 1.30 on graded exposure compared to an effect size of 1.10 on antidepressant medication; Christiansen, Hadzi-Pavlovic, Andrews and Mattick (1987) studied OCD being treated with exposure based treatments and found an effect size of 1.37. The Quality Assurance Project (1985) found effect sizes of .98 with behavioral treatments for anxiety and 1.37 with exposure therapies for obsessive-compulsive behaviors. In reviewing a meta-analysis of 43 studies for panic disorder

(Gould, Otto, & Pollack, 1995) comparing CBT with pharmacological and combined CBT/pharmacological treatments, CBT was found to have fewer drop-out rates (5.6%), than either pharmacological treatments (19.8%) or combined CBT/pharmacological treatments (22.0%). Additionally, CBT produced larger effect sizes (.68) than pharmacological treatments (.47) and combined treatments (.56). In their meta-analytic review of a variety of treatments for anxiety disorders, Lambert and Ogles (2004) concluded that "psychotherapies clearly show effectiveness compared to wait list and no treatment control comparison groups."

## EVIDENCED-BASED TREATMENTS FOR ANXIETY DISORDERS IN COLLEGE MENTAL HEALTH

Campus based therapists wanting to know the EBT literature in our field would likely be disappointed by the scarcity of outcome research on anxiety disorders in college mental health. Moreover, the majority of the existing empirical evidence in college settings is based on non-clinical samples, especially psychology student volunteers. And, most of the research focuses on understanding other important variables such as assessing the relationship between OCD and treatment issues (Spengler, 1998); anxiety disorders and other co-morbid disorders such as PTSD and alcohol consumption (Huppert, Gershung, Riggs, Spokas, Filip, Hajcak, Parkar, Baer, & Foa, 2004; Kidorf & Lang, 1999); examining group difference among social phobia subtypes (McNeil, Vrana, Melamed, Cuthbert, & Lang, 1993); the impact of anxiety disorders on educational achievement (Ameringen, Mancini, & Farvolden, 2003); psychometric properties of the OCI-R in a college sample (Hajcak, Huppert, Simons, & Foa, 2004) and the traumatization of college students with the September 11 attacks (Blanchard, Kuhn, Rowell, Hickling, Wittrock, Rogers, Johnson, & Steckler, 2004; Blanchard, Rowell, Kuhn, Rogers, & Wittrock, 2004).

As noted above, outcomes studies with college students are often limited to volunteers or students in psychology courses and generally lack the research rigor expected from Empirically Supported Treatments (ESTs). Consequently, few findings of significance emerge. For example, two studies conducted in college contexts examined eye-movement desensitization and reprocessing (EMDR) for public speaking anxiety (Carrigan & Levis, 1999) and fear of spiders (Bates, McGlynn, Montgomery, & Mattke, 1996) reported non-significant outcomes. In the first study, investigators isolated the effects of EMDR from the use of imagery alone. They utilized a variety of outcome measures, including physiological measures, but found no evidence for the effect of any of the treatments on the reduction of public speaking fears of undergraduate students. In the second study, Bates and his colleagues studied the effects of EMDR versus no treatment on pre-post treatment measures concerning reductions in the fear of spiders. Again, they found no evidence that EMDR led to significant change.

However, some university mental health focused investigations have reported gains from therapy (see Table 2). Borkovec, Mathews, Chambless, Ebrahimi, Lytle and Nelson (1987) found significant results for the treatment of generalized anxiety disorder with a combination of relaxation training and cognitive therapy. Register, Beckham, May, and Gustafson (1991) reported positive treatment outcomes through the use of stress inoculation bibliotherapy with test anxious undergraduate college students. His study involved minimal therapist contact (phone) and used a stress inoculation treatment manual that included procedures for relaxation training, cognitive coping strategies, and imaginal exposure. Also, Valdez (2003), in another study (unpublished master's thesis), compared Anglo American versus Mexican American college students and found cognitive restructuring to be equally efficacious with both groups in reducing worry about their academic careers. Finally, in a pilot test of counseling center college students with public speaking fears (Baez, 2003), graduate students were treated with a manualized CBT and In-Vivo Psychodrama-Based Desensitization (IVPBD) approach in a group format for 6 weeks. Results of pre-post testing with social anxiety and public speaking apprehension measures were significant and positive. This may suggest that eclectic approaches that utilize specific tested techniques can be effective and useful in providing the clinician with some flexibility to address specific problems and enhancing the effectiveness of the treatments. In addition, given the high demand for counseling services, college students may benefit from outreach programs (e.g., web based programs, classes, workshops, etc.) geared towards teaching stress inoculation and other CBT strategies early in their college years. Supporting evidence for this can be found in Lambert, Rietdijik, Hudcovicova, Van de Ven, Schrieken, and Emmelkamp (2003) where in a controlled randomized trial of the treatment of PTSD through the internet, they found positive results on the internet treatment condition in comparison to a waiting-list control group.

TABLE 2. Evidenced-Based Supportive Interventions for Anxiety Disorders in College Mental Health

| Anxiety Disorders Classification | Evidenced-Based Supportive Treatments | Authors |
|---|---|---|
| Generalized Anxiety Disorder | Relaxation plus Cognitive Therapy | (Borkovec et al., 1987) |
| | Cognitive Restructuring with Anglo American & Mexican American college students | (Valdez, 2003) |
| Specific Phobias | EMDR (Fear of Spiders) Non-significant* | (Bates et al., 1996) |
| | EMDR (Fear of Public Speaking) *Non-significant | (Carrigan & Levis, 1999) |
| | Stress Inoculation | |
| | Bibliotherapy (Test Anxiety) | (Register et al., 1991) |
| | Group CBT & Psychodrama (Fear of Public Speaking) | (Baez, 2003, unpublished) |

## EVIDENCE FOR THERAPIST/RELATIONSHIP FACTORS IN PSYCHOTHERAPY OUTCOMES OF ANXIETY DISORDERS

The general psychology literature suggests that therapist/relationship factors (common factors) account for 30% of the variance in outcome studies while specific techniques account for 15% of the variance (Lambert, 1992). Studies looking at the therapy relationship and common factors in the area of anxiety disorders, although important, are scarce. One recent study (Huppert et al., 2004) found that therapist efficacy contributed to outcome in CBT treatment for Panic disorder and that overall experience (avg., 8.9 years) in conducting psychotherapy contributed positively to outcome as well. In addition, Miller, Taylor, and West (1980) in a follow-up study comparing the effectiveness of various behavioral approaches with problem drinkers, found that the therapists' rank on empathy accounted for 67% of the variance with patient outcomes suggesting that therapist factors in psychotherapy outcomes are more important than the specific therapeutic intervention or mental condition. No specific studies on common factors in the treatment of anxiety disorders for university students receiving services at college counseling centers were found.

## CHALLENGES AND SUGGESTIONS
## FOR CONDUCTING OUTCOME RESEARCH
## ON ANXIETY DISORDERS IN COLLEGE MENTAL HEALTH

Given the limitation of the generalizability of results of the current efficacy studies on anxiety disorders treatment to our university communities, counseling center professionals need to adapt and tailor the Evidenced-Based Practices (EBPs) to fit our student characteristics and environment. More importantly, we need to conduct research within our context. The following five categories for planning and organizing effectiveness studies in college mental health settings may be helpful.

The first component is development of a vision/plan for EBP anxiety reduction research. Suggestions are to:

1. develop partnerships with colleagues and with other centers and universities;
2. develop a long term vision of a research plan;
3. keep up to date on the recent outcome research related to your area of research;
4. enlist the support of your administrators (e.g., director) for protected time, resources, etc.;
5. watch out for situations causing splitting or multiple role conflict between the roles you serve as a clinician versus as a researcher (Johnson & Remien, 2003);
6. be creative about developing studies that fit the needs of the clients, agency and research;
7. consider other ways of examining what we already do, such as sophisticated qualitative methods;
8. accept that in our clinical practice, we treat the whole person. (This requires clinical flexibility such that the client's issues could be addressed outside of the study through another therapist or counselor.)

The second component for conducting EBP anxiety reduction research consists of several procedural actions. Probable steps include:

1. attempt to get your study exempt when seeking Institutional Review Board (IRB) approval from the university;
2. know that for IRB approval, if your study includes minors and you ordinarily don't get parental consent for treatment for these students, you may not need to obtain such parental consent for the study since student written consent (except for those under 18) may be sufficient;
3. advertise through the media of e-mail avoiding key strategic periods (e.g., not at the beginning of the semester when students are overloaded with information);
4. consider using web site private servers that protect confidentiality plus make it easier for students to follow-up at the end of treatment;
5. consider writing the results for publication during the summer months when college counseling centers typically aren't as busy.

The next component needed for conducting efficacy studies of evidence-based anxiety reduction in college mental health involves design considerations:

1. use a benchmarking research strategy by comparing the magnitudes of change obtained in the efficacy studies (McFall, 1996; Wade, Treat, & Stuart, 1998);
2. use pre-post testing employing well validated measures;
3. use an informational session to conduct pre-testing and to randomly assign students to control or treatment groups, beginning with the treatment groups and, once the group is completed, administer the treatment to the control group. (If the treatment is brief, e.g., 6 weeks or less, you can run both groups in one semester.);
4. if you are offering a research group that includes a control group, you may need to offer individual therapy if the student cannot or should not wait;
5. train graduate students to conduct the treatment, so that you can be blind to influence as to whom receives the treatment;
6. separate the names from the testing instruments so that you do not know who is in the study and who is not. (As yet another step, have another colleague or student collect the data.);
7. use brief valid instruments such as the Beck Depression Inventory (BDI) (Beck, Steer, & Garbin, 1988), in between sessions to determine therapy outcome, or examine the therapeutic allegiance

through the Working Alliance Inventory (WAI) (Horvath & Greenberg, 1989);

8. pre-determine the boundaries of the clinical contacts and the range of interventions that would be provided in order not to deter from the treatment protocols (Johnson & Remien, 2003).

Training implications are often another important consideration with EBP anxiety disorders investigations. Four options are:

1. consider tape-recording the sessions in order to insure the accountability and integrity of the research focus. Be it on interventions or process factors;
2. use the tape-recordings directly for training or supervision purposes (Johnson & Remien, 2003);
3. provide staff/intern development presentations on the results of the study;
4. use the research project to train staff/interns on the importance of transporting the evidenced-based treatments into the clinical setting.

Finally, certain ethical considerations for EBP anxiety reduction studies are critical:

1. inform clients that they are not required to be part of the study in order to receive the treatment because the center would be providing the treatment anyway;
2. make the boundaries between therapist and researcher roles versus the client and research participant roles clear to students and staff.

## *SUGGESTIONS FOR CLINICAL WORK*
## *WITH CHRONICALLY ANXIOUS COLLEGE STUDENTS*

Students seeking help at college counseling centers tend to experience anxiety at both predictable and unpredictable times, ranging from predictable reactions to trauma (e.g., sexual assault) and specific situations that make them feel nervous (e.g., tests, oral presentations, meeting new people, etc.) to unpredictable situations such as waking up afraid in the middle of the night in a panic-like manner and not knowing why. Since students often present with multiple issues, anxiety may be disguised as other presenting concerns, for example, abusing alcohol or using other drugs to manage social anxiety; increased depression due to frustration of not being able to cope with anxiety; or poorer grades due to not being able to participate or speak in class, test well, or pass oral comprehensive exams. As a result, it is important to begin with a broad clinical interview. Testing, using a general spectrum inventory such as the Outcome Questionnaire (OQ-45) (Lambert, Hansen, Umphress, Lunnen, Okiishi, Burlingame, Huefner, & Reisinger, 1996) or the Brief Symptom Inventory (BSI) (Derogatis, 1993), should also be considered. Alternative assessment indices may include the self-help type questionnaires on the web that are under the public domain.

Once a diagnosis or conceptualization of the presenting anxiety problems is completed, treatment can begin. However, it is a generally recognized practice to treat first conditions associated with potentially harmful behaviors such as suicidality or alcohol dependency. Similarly, it may be advisable in certain cases to refer to a medical doctor for a physical exam to rule out any medical concerns. Initially, students typically benefit by receiving something that provides some immediate relief such as a basic relaxation strategy (e.g., diaphragmatic breathing) or being able to talk about what they are going through. It is often helpful to let them know that anxiety is a condition that can be treated successfully with individual or group psychotherapy (e.g., CBT) alone or with medication. Another important strategy can be to provide information on the nature of the anxiety and how anxiety produces the physiological symptoms (e.g., heart racing, shallow breathing, trembling, etc.). Other helpful information may include explanations of the fight-flight response, the relationship between anxiety and performance, and the need to focus on managing the anxiety rather than eliminating it.

College counselors might consider encouraging students to gather data through journaling about specific symptoms and their severity, how long they last, under what conditions they occur, and how the student has tried to cope. Generally, as clients gather and record such data, they become more aware of the precipitating events, which may assist them to talk about what types of thoughts seem to go along when the anxiety is about to occur or is occurring. As a result, most students using journaling would understand that their anxiety does not occur due to particular activating events but due to their perceptions of the events or irrational thoughts (e.g., through CBT). As clients continue to log the events and the irrational thoughts, it is likely that they would perceive an increase in their irrational thinking. At this time, the college counseling center therapist might suggest that the increase is not necessarily due to the symptoms getting worse but to the fact that they are better at recognizing them and, that eventually, the symptoms almost always decrease with treatment. As students continue to use CBT strategies by disputing irrational thoughts, correcting cognitive distortions, learning response prevention, practicing progressive muscle relaxation and imagery exercises, their co-morbidity symptoms usually decrease as well. Finally, it is important to remind clients that if they stop practicing the strategies too soon, the symptoms may return. Providing or being available for a follow-up or booster sessions at a later time can be very helpful to maintain or enhance gains.

## FUTURE DIRECTIONS AND QUESTIONS FOR RESEARCH AND PRACTICE WITH ANXIETY DISORDERS

As a scientist practitioner who works in college mental health, I believe the seven principles of empirically supported interventions in counseling psychology (Wampold, 2002), have utility in the research of EBP with anxiety disorders, especially the guidelines for relative efficacy (principle 4), outcomes assessed at the local setting (principle 7), and recognition of the freedom of choice in adapting interventions (principle 7). These two principles reflect the importance of adjusting treatments for anxiety problems based on our particular respective clinical settings and recognition of the clinical decision making of competent clinicians while maintaining rigorous methodology. As it has been suggested by Benton, Robertson, Tseng, Newton, and Benton (2003), college counseling centers today are dealing with increased chronicity, co-morbidity, and complexity of issues yet with the same or less professional resources.

Efficacy research on client anxiety reduction is much needed in college mental health. Given the limitation of resources, more partnerships should be developed similar to those already in place, including The Research Consortium of Counseling and Psychological Services at the Counseling and Mental Health Center at The University of Texas in Austin, and Suffolk University among others (See Counseling Center Village web page at (http://ubcounseling.buffalo.edu/rn.html). Also, more governmental support is needed, such as what was envisioned with the "Garrett Lee Smith Memorial Act" (The Counseling Center Care Bill) (APA, 2004) which, if funded, could provide college counseling centers with more financial resources to conduct empirically supported outcome research.

There are challenges to conducting such EBP anxiety disorders research due to requirements for achieving rigorous protocols competing against the practical clinical needs of the college counseling center of today. Among others, the rigor imposed by clinical trials requires manualized treatments, specificity of diagnosis, and using reliable outcome instruments. University mental health services are typically eclectic, avoid diagnosis but are poly-problem oriented, and may lack the resources to purchase high quality outcome instruments. Many counseling centers may also have to deal with constraints imposed by institutional review boards (IRB) and the national HIPPA guidelines, the need for increased service delivery, and no research time allotment for clinicians.

Given the nationwide public recognition of major mental health concerns (e.g., anxiety, suicide, substance abuse, and others) among college students across the nation, university mental health centers are becoming more visible and their impact on the university is widely recognized. Enough seems to be known about the treatment of anxiety disorders to suggest that we can be effective in assisting most students who seek our services for these problems. Student mental health services centers are a vital source of support for students with these disorders so that they can function and excel in the stressful academic environment.

## CONCLUSIONS

Empirically supported treatments for anxiety disorders appear to have been fruitful in demonstrating treatments that are efficacious for specific conditions. These treatment approaches tend to be based on cognitive, behavioral, and CBT strategies which are active and brief in line with the present trends in college mental health toward symptom focused and time limited practices. Nevertheless, the available efficacy research may have uncertain clinical utility or may lack in generalizability to transport them to our student populations. Moreover, the efficacy research on anxiety disorders in counseling mental health centers is especially scarce.

Given the stringent measures and lack of generalizability of Empirically Supported Treatments (ESTs), what appears to be lacking in college counseling center research are excellently designed investigations on the process of how people change. What many practitioners notice, as I have, is that factors other than prescribed interventions also appear to be quite meaningful and worthy of empirical research. These other factors include the strength of the therapeutic relationship, cohesion, and the installation of hope by the therapist. Given that as much as 30% of the variance in treatment outcome may be accounted for by therapist/ relationship factors, investigations of these factors are likely to be important to the work of counselors in college counseling centers.

With nationwide public recognition and financial support for mental health services, college counseling centers can increase the delivery of brief and competent services to students, while producing outcome research that is tailored to our particular population. Also, we can develop outcome-based outreach programming to influence our student environments while contributing to the knowledge of evidenced-based practices.

In summary, with an expanded view of evidence (Chwalisz, 2003) and the interplay of science and practice informing each other, we can improve our ability to provide competent services to our students in the area of anxiety prevention and anxiety disorders remediation. Additionally, it is important that we develop training on ESTs, both didactic and experiential, for our future college counseling centers clinicians and the profession at large. This requires us to begin with the professional development of current mid-level and senior clinicians, so that they can integrate the EST knowledge base with their wisdom in clinical practice, and then train and mentor interns with this perspective.

## REFERENCES

American Psychological Association, Public Policy Office (2004). *Congressional update: Garrett Lee Smith memorial act passes house and senate*. Retrieved November 1, 2004 from http://www.apa.org/ppo/eglsupdt904.html

Ameringen, M. V., Mancini, C., & Farvolden, P. (2003). The impact of anxiety disorders on educational achievement. *Journal of Anxiety Disorders, 17*(5), 561-571.

Andrews, G. (1982). A methodology for preparing "ideal" treatment outlines in psychiatry. *The Australian and New Zealand Journal of Psychiatry, 16*, 153-158.

Anxiety Disorders Association of America. (2003). *Statistics and facts about anxiety disorders. Anxiety Disorders Association of America*. Retrieved July, 1, 2004 from http://adaa.org/mediaroom/index.cfm

Baez, T. (2003). *A CBT and psychodrama based treatment group for public speaking anxiety with college students*. Unpublished manuscript, University of Michigan.

Bates, L. W., McGlynn, F. D., Montgomery, R. W., & Mattke, T. (1996). Effects of eye-movement desensitization versus no treatment on repeated measures of fear of spiders. *Journal of Anxiety Disorders, 10*(6), 555-569.

Beck, A.T., Steer, R.A., & Garbin, M.G. (1988). Psychometric properties of the Beck Depression Inventory: Twenty-five years of evaluation. *Clinical Psychology Review, 8*(1), 77-100.

Benton, S.A., Benton, S.L., Newton, F.B., Beton, K.L. & Robertson, J.M. (2004). Changes in client's problems: Contributions and limitations from a 13-year study. *Professional Psychology: Research and Practice, 35*(3), 317-319.

Blanchard, E. B., Kuhn, E., Rowell, D. L., Hickling, E. J., Wittrock, D., Rogers, R. L., Johnson, M. R., & Steckler, D. C. (2004). Studies of the vicarious traumatization of college students by the September 11th attacks: Effects of proximity, exposure and connectedness. *Behaviour Research and Therapy, 42*(2), 191-205.

Blanchard, E. B., Rowell, D., Kuhn, E., Rogers, R., & Wittrock, D. (2004). Post-traumatic stress and depressive symptoms in a college population one year after the September 11 attacks: The effect of proximity. *Behaviour Research and Therapy, 43*(1), 143-150.

Borkovec, T. D., Mathews, A. M., Chambers, A., Ebrahimi, S., Lytle, R., & Nelson, R. (1987). The effects of relaxation training with cognitive or nondirective therapy and the role of relaxation-induced anxiety in the treatment of general anxiety. *Journal of Consulting and Clinical Psychology, 55*(6), 883-888.

Carrigan, M. H., & Levis, D. J. (1999). The Contributions of Eye Movements to the Efficacy of Brief Exposure Treatment for Reducing Fear of Public Speaking. *Journal of Anxiety Disorders, 13*(1-2), 101-118.

Chambless, D. L. (2002). Identification of empirically supported counseling psychology interventions: Commentary. *The Counseling Psychologist, 30*(2), 302-308.

Chambless, D. L. & Ollendick, T. H. (2001). Empirically supported psychological interventions: Controversies and evidence. *Annual Review of Psychology, 52,* 685-716.

Chiles, J. A., Lambert, M. J., & Hatch, A. L. (1999). The impact of psychological interventions on medical cost offset: A meta-analytic review. *Clinical Psychology: Science and Practice, 6,* 204-220.

Christiansen, H., Hadzi-Pavlovic, D., Andrews, G., & Mattick, R. (1987). Behavior therapy and tricyclic medication in the treatment of obsessive-compulsive disorder: A quantitative review. *Journal of Consulting and Clinical Psychology, 55*(5), 701-711.

Chwalisz, K. (2003). Evidenced-based practice: A framework for twenty-first-century science-practitioner training. *The Counseling Psychologist, 31*(5), 497-528.

Derogatis, L.R. (1993). *BSI: Administration, scoring, and procedures manual* (3rd ed.) Minneapolis, MN: National Computer Systems.

Hajcak, G., Huppert, J. D., Simons, R. F., & Foa, E. B. (2004). Psychometric properties of the OCI-R in a college sample. *Behaviour Research and Therapy, 42*(1), 115-123.

Horvath, A.O. & Greenberg, L.S. (1989). Development and validation of the Working Alliance Inventory. *Journal of Counseling Psychology, 36*(2), 223-233.

Huppert, J. D., Moser, J. S., Gershuny, B. S., Riggs, D. S., Spokas, M., Filip, J., Hajcak, G., Parkar, A., Baer, L., & Foa, E. (2004). The relationship between obsessive-compulsive and posttraumatic stress symptoms in clinical and non-clinical samples. *Journal of Anxiety Disorders, 19*(1), 127-136.

Johnson, M. O. & Remien, R. H. (2003). Adherence to research protocols in a clinical context: Challenges and recommendations from behavioral intervention trials. *American Journal of Psychotherapy, 57*(3), 348-360.

Kidorf, M. &. Lang, A. R. (1999). Effects of social anxiety and alcohol expectancies on stress-induced drinking. *Psychology of Addictive Behaviors, 13*(2), 134-142.

Lambert, M. J. (1992). Psychotherapy outcome research. In J. C. Norcross & M. R. Goldfried (Eds.), *Handbook of psychotherapy integration*. (pp. 94-129). New York: Basic Books.

Lambert, M.J., Hansen, N.B., Umphress, V.J., Lunnen, K., Okiishi, J., Burlingame, G.M., Huefner, J.C., & Reisinger, C.W. (1996). *Administration and scoring manual for the Outcome Questionnaire (OQ-45)*. Wilmington, DE: American Professional Credentialing Services.

Lambert, M. J. & Ogles, B. M. (2004). The efficacy and effectiveness of psychotherapy. In M. J. Lambert (Ed.), *Bergin and Garfield's Handbook of Psychotherapy and Behavior Change* (pp. 139-193). New York: Wiley.

Lange, A., Rietdijk, D., Hudcovicoca, M., Van de Ven, J-P., Schrieken, B. & Emmelkamp, P.M.G. (2003). Interapy: A controlled randomized trial of the standard treatment of posttraumatic stress through the internet. *Journal of Consulting and Clinical Psychology, 71*(5), 901-909.

McFall, R. M. (1996). Consumer satisfaction as a way of evaluating psychotherapy: Ecological validity and all that versus the good old randomized trial (panel discussion). 6th annual convention of the American Association of Applied and Preventative Psychology, San Francisco.

McNeil, D. W., Vrana, S. R., Melamed, B. G., Cuthbert, B. N., & Lang, P. J. (1993). Emotional Imagery in Simple and Social Phobia: Fear versus Anxiety. *Journal of Abnormal Psychology, 102*(2), 212-235.

Miller, W. R., Taylor, C. A., & West, J. C. (1980). Focused versus broad-spectrum behavior therapy for problem drinkers. *Journal of Consulting and Clinical Psychology, 48*, 590-601.

Nathan, P. E., & Gorman, J. M. (Eds.). (2002). *A guide to treatments that work* (2nd ed.). New York: Oxford University Press.

Olfson, M., Marcus, S.C., Wan, G.J., & Geissler, E.C. (2004). National trends in the outpatient treatment of anxiety disorders. *Journal of Clinical Psychiatry, 65*(9), 1166-1173.

Quality Assurance Project. (1985). Treatment of outlines for the management of anxiety states. *Australian and New Zealand Journal of Psychiatry, 19*, 138-151.

Register, A. C., Beckham, J. C., May, J. G., & Gustafson, D. J. (1991). Stress Inoculation Bibliotherapy in the Treatment of Test Anxiety. *Journal of Counseling Psychology, 38*(2), 115-119.

Spengler, P. M. (1998). Assessment and treatment of obsessive-compulsive behavior in college age students and adults. *Journal of Mental Health Counseling, 20*(2), 95-111.

Valdez, G. (2003). Comparing the relative efficacy of cognitive restructuring between Anglo American and Mexican American college students. Unpublished master's thesis. University of Texas, Austin, Texas.

Wade, W. A., Treat, T. A., & Stuart, G. L. (1998). Transporting an empirically supported treatment for panic disorder to a service clinic setting: A benchmark strategy. *Journal of Consulting and Clinical Psychology, 66*(20), 231-239.

Wampold, B. E., Lichtenberg, J. W., & Waehler, C. A. (2002). Principles of empirically supported interventions in counseling psychology. *The Counseling Psychologist. 30*(2), 197-217.

# Chapter 5.
# Evidence-Based Practice
# for Treatment of Eating Disorders

## Jaquelyn Liss Resnick

**SUMMARY.** The purpose of this chapter is to review the status of evidence-based practice (EBP) for the treatment of students with eating disorders in university and college counseling centers. Several issues affecting the application of the research findings to service delivery for eating disordered students will be addressed. These include discussion of EBP research paradigms, populations studied, treatment interventions selected, other salient variables examined, utilization of appropriate assessment indices and meaningful outcome measures, and multicultural considerations. EBP relevant guidelines, implications and suggestions for future directions in college mental health are presented. *[Article copies available for a fee from The Haworth Document Delivery Service: 1-800-HAWORTH. E-mail address: <docdelivery@haworthpress.com> Website: <http://www.HaworthPress.com> © 2005 by The Haworth Press, Inc. All rights reserved.]*

**KEYWORDS.** Eating disorders, evidence-based practice, college mental health, anorexia nervosa, bulimia nervosa, eating disorder NOS, binge eating disorder

---

Jaquelyn Liss Resnick, PhD, is Director and Professor at the University of Florida Counseling Center, PO Box 114100, Gainesville, FL 32611-4100 (E-mail: resnick@counsel.ufl.edu).

[Haworth co-indexing entry note]: "Chapter 5. Evidence-Based Practice for Treatment of Eating Disorders" Resnick, Jaquelyn Liss. Co-published simultaneously in *Journal of College Student Psychotherapy* (The Haworth Press, Inc.) Vol. 20, No. 1, 2005, pp. 49-65; and: *Evidence-Based Psychotherapy Practice in College Mental Health* (ed: Stewart E. Cooper) The Haworth Press, Inc., 2005, pp. 49-65. Single or multiple copies of this article are available for a fee from The Haworth Document Delivery Service [1-800-HAWORTH, 9:00 a.m. - 5:00 p.m. (EST). E-mail address: docdelivery@haworthpress.com].

The purpose of this chapter is to provide an overview of the current status of evidence-based practice (EBP) for the treatment of students with eating disorders in university and college counseling centers. EBP paradigms can be made useful for campus-based practice. The EBP movement is driven by scientific inquiry, the search for best practices and the consideration of stakeholders' interests, including clients, health care providers, and institutional or other third party payers. At best, EBP involves a focus on accountability, with principal goals to demonstrate that psychotherapy effectiveness stands up to empirical scrutiny and that practice is informed by scientific findings. At worst, EBP elicits concerns about the misuse of EBP data by Managed Care and other third party payers in ways that would limit or hurt health care service delivery. The roots of the EBP movement stem from the medical model calling for empirically validated treatments with controlled clinical trials, carefully monitored interventions, and dosage effects testing for specific diagnoses.

In the application of empirically validated treatments to the realm of counseling and psychotherapy, however, significant questions arise as to what constitutes replicable interventions, reliable evidence, and appropriate measures to evaluate the efficacy of treatments. Perhaps as one consequence of this uncertainty, the framework of what should be included is ever broadening. The language used reflects this evolution, moving from empirically validated treatment (EVT) to empirically based treatment (EBT) to empirically supported interventions (ESI) and empirically supported relationships (ESR) and now to evidence-based practice (EBP), evidence informed practice (EIP), and evidence informed interventions (EII) (Barlow, 2000; Chambless & Hollon, 1998; Norcross, 2001; Wampold, Lichtenberg & Waehler, 2002). For purposes of this chapter, the term evidence-based practice (EBP) will be used as an umbrella reference for all of these terms. Later in this chapter, unique aspects of college counseling centers will be elucidated as they differ from the practice sites where most EBP research has taken place.

## EATING DISORDERS

Most counselors in university and college counseling centers deal with at least some clients with a diagnosis of mild, moderate, or severe eating disorders as large numbers of female students (and a much smaller number of males) present with such concerns. Eating disorders are characterized by severe disturbances in eating behavior, with definitions typically based on the *Diagnostic and Statistical Manual of Mental Disorders (DSM-IV-TR)* (American Psychiatric Association, 2000): Anorexia Nervosa (AN), Bulimia Nervosa (BN), and Eating Disorder Not Otherwise Specified (EDNOS) are the three major subtypes with Binge Eating Disorder (BED) representing a newer category being investigated. The treatment of obesity is not addressed in this article, since obesity is considered by the *DSM-IV-TR* (American Psychiatric Association, 2000) to be a medical disorder not consistently associated with psychological syndrome or behavior; however, obesity may be co-morbid with BED.

The findings of EBP studies regarding eating disorders vary by specific diagnosis. Eating disorders were first included in the *DSM-III* (American Psychiatric Association, 1980). The revised editions contain different criteria for eating disorders with increasing levels of severity and greater specificity required for diagnosis. Many clients presenting to university and college counseling centers may not meet the strict criteria for AN or BN and more frequently fit the EDNOS classification, which is not surprising, since eating disorders are often thought to exist along a continuum, varying in severity rather than occurring in discrete categories (Herzog & Delinsky, 2002). Eating disorders affect approximately 10% of adolescent girls and women, making them some of the most gendered diagnoses in the *DSM* (Smolak & Murnen, 2002). It should be noted that regardless of the eating disorder diagnosis, little EBP research has actually been conducted in college counseling center settings.

### Anorexia Nervosa

AN is characterized in the *DSM-IV-TR* (American Psychiatric Association, 2000) by refusal to maintain minimally normal body weight, intense fear of becoming fat, distorted perception of body size or shape, with amenorrhea in postmenarcheal females. Two AN subtypes are noted: Restricting and Bingeing/Purging. There is little research on outcomes for treatment, especially in outpatient settings such as university mental health services. Wilson and Fairburn (2002) suggest that this lack of studies in outpatient contexts may be due to the low incidence of the disorder, the clinical and methodological difficulties inherent in studying AN (including small potential samples and difficulty to engage in treatment), and the severity of these problems, which may require hospitalization.

Stein, Saelens, Dounchis, Lewczk, Swenson and Wilfley (2001) describe a small number of controlled studies based of AN on Euro-American females in their mid to late teens. Primary favorable outcomes include weight gain and resumed menstruation. They also reported a few studies involving family therapy that have demonstrated some effectiveness, although it is difficult to draw conclusions from such a small number of investigations. The applicability of a family therapy model in a college or university counseling center is limited, since students are often geographically separated from family. Cognitive-behavioral therapy (CBT) has recently been studied for AN with promising but limited findings (Wilson, 1999). Studies to date have not clearly established a role for pharmacotherapy (Wilson & Fairburn, 2002). Due to the complex medical consequences of AN, including a significant mortality rate, college counseling center practitioners should work closely with physicians and nutritionists in providing outpatient treatment, an essential collaboration which nevertheless complicates evaluating treatment within the EBP paradigm. It is difficult to generalize or identify effective treatments for AN because of these multiple research constraints.

### Bulimia Nervosa

The *DSM-IV-TR* (American Psychiatric Association, 2000) describes the essential features of BN as binge eating, inappropriate compensatory methods to prevent weight gain (bingeing and purging or using other compensatory behaviors such as laxative abuse, excessive exercise or fasting at least twice a week for 3 months), and self-evaluation excessively influenced by body shape and weight. Two BN subtypes are noted: Purging and Nonpurging. BN is the most studied among the eating disorders (Wilson & Fairburn, 2002) though again, relatively few EBP investigations have taken place in university mental health services contexts. Primary outcome measures are frequency of bingeing and purging or other compensatory behaviors. Study samples remain predominantly Euro-American females in their early 20's presenting without co-morbidity (Stein et al., 2001).

The most intensely studied BN treatment is CBT that addresses the presenting behaviors of bingeing and purging as well the extreme dietary restraint and dysfunctional thoughts and attitudes about idealized body shape and weight (Wilson, 1997). The cognitive model suggests that treatment may also need to address negative self-evaluation, perfectionism and dichotomous thinking, and perhaps also the ability to tolerate negative affect. The cognitive conceptual framework posits that vulnerable women, often college students, idealize thinness and unrealistically restrict their food in pursuit of this goal leading to periodic loss of control over eating (bingeing) and then purging as an attempt to compensate and reduce anxiety. A vicious cycle of distress and lower self-esteem leads to increased reliance on the drive to be thinner, even more restrictive eating, and another binge/purge cycle.

Manual based CBT uses an integrated sequence of cognitive and behavioral interventions that typically begin with psychoeducational and behavioral interventions, then move to cognitive interventions, and finally conclude with interventions aimed at maintenance of change over time. Reviewing a number of well designed studies with over 20 controlled trials for CBT showing some efficacy, Wilson and Fairburn (2002) conclude that manual-based CBT is first line treatment of choice for BN (with about half ceasing binge and purge behaviors). They note that CBT is well accepted by the majority of patients, is effective in eliminating core features, and often improves co-morbid problems such as low self-esteem and depression; and long-term positive effects seem reasonably stable.

Wilson and Fairburn (2002) note that CBT may be more effective in treatment of specific bulimic symptoms but not more effective than alternative treatments in dealing with associated aspects of BN such as personal well-being or relational effectiveness. Interpersonal Psychotherapy (IPT) is the alternative intervention most often studied. IPT helps clients identify and modify current interpersonal problems, and identifies their link to eating behavior (Stein et al., 2001). The treatment phases include: (1) identification of the most significant interpersonal problems areas; (2) changing functioning in those areas; and (3) a termination phase consolidating therapeutic work and preparing client for further independent work. IPT treatment typically spans 15-20 sessions.

A treatment approach that takes into account a more complex model is proposed by Wonderlich, Mitchell, Peterson, and Crow (2002) and is referred to as Integrative Cognitive Therapy (ICT). ICT may be highly suitable for work with college clients. ICT looks at emotional states as proximal antecedents for binge eating and with bulimic behavior as an effort to regulate or escape from negative affect. ICT is an extension of CBT that incorporates affective, cultural and biological factors. It takes into account that BN clients are more likely to have events that threaten the attachment process such as more physical and sexual abuse in childhood, parental histories of psychopathology, and conflictual, disengaged and non-nurturant families of origin. Four treatment phases are delineated in ICT: (1) education using a workbook; (2) normalization of eating and associated coping skills; (3) exploration of interpersonal patterns and schemas; and, (4) relapse prevention and lifestyle management. Again, approximately 20 sessions are employed in the manualized version of this intervention. The ICT model is promising, especially for the treatment of college students with BN, but it is still in its early stage of development and requires further testing.

A few studies have examined a Stepped-Care approach to BN, which sequences interventions based on intensity, cost and efficacy, progressing from self-help to therapist intervention; clients begin with the least intense and expensive treatment, and move up steps as needed (Stein et al., 2001; Wilson, Vitiusek & Loeb, 2000). Initial investigations of the Stepped-Care approach have suggested some positive outcomes but further studies are required before conclusions can be drawn.

Wilson and Fairburn (2002) reviewed the literature that examined the effect of antidepressant medication for BN, with and without other psychotherapy. Several classes of antidepressant drugs produced greater reductions in bingeing and purging in the short term in BN than placebo; however, the long term results remain mostly untested and the effects when combined with psychotherapeutic interventions are mixed. Comparisons of CBT and antidepressant drugs indicate that CBT is more acceptable to patients than medication, the dropout rate is lower, and the treatment is superior to drugs alone; combining CBT with medication is more effective than medication alone but produces few consistent benefits over CBT alone, although combining might aid in reducing co-morbid anxiety and depression (Wilson & Fairburn, 2002, p. 565).

The severity and complexity involved in BN and its treatment pose a challenge when examining the utility of EBP findings, both for the general population and for the college student client population. Clearly CBT and IPT provide some positive results, with CBT found to be equal or superior to all treatments to which it has been compared (Wilson, 1997). Nevertheless, success here still means that up to 50 percent do not see a reduction in binge/purge behaviors. Thus, for the clients who derive little or no benefit from those interventions, other treatment strategies must be considered. Few clinical treatment studies examine more integrative orientations such as ICT or consider different interventions for stages of treatment. For example, group therapy as a primary or adjunctive treatment modality for those at the action stage of change has not been well studied.

## Eating Disorder Not Otherwise Specified

The EDNOS category refers to eating disorders that do not meet criteria for AN or BN. For example, EDNOS includes someone who meets all the criteria for BN but at a sub-morbid frequency. In actual practice, many students present at college counseling centers with an eating disorder that takes an "atypical" form. Herzog and Delinsky (2002) note that contrary to being atypical, the EDNOS diagnosis is common, given to from 25 percent to 50 percent of clients who present with disordered eating. Unfortunately, most EBP studies exclude subjects who do not present with pure *DSM-IV-TR* diagnosis for AN or BN, so little can be said about interventions for EDNOS. The one exception is Binge Eating Disorder (BED), introduced in 1994 as a provisional category requiring further study, and currently classified as EDNOS in the *DSM-IV-TR* (American Psychiatric Association, 2000).

## Binge Eating Disorder

According to the *DSM-IV-TR*, research criteria for the provisional BED diagnosis include recurrent episodes of binge eating with impaired control and significant distress over bingeing, and the absence of purging or other inappropriate compensatory behaviors at least twice a week for at least six months (American Psychiatric Association, 2000). Prevalence is 0.7 percent to 4 percent of the general population, with 30 percent in weight control programs. Onset is typically in late adolescence. BED is 1.5 times more likely for women than men and may be co-morbid with obesity.

Treatment of BED has focused on management of weight and eating behavior. Studies have looked at CBT, IPT, pharmacological, behavioral weight loss (BWL), and Stepped-Care programs. Studies report problems with adherence, drop out, and relapse rates with all five of the above programs. Most investigations were conducted outside of campus-based practice settings. At this juncture, no treatment has proved differentially effective with small sample sizes and the focus on very short term results limiting current findings (Wilson & Fairburn, 2002; Stein et al., 2001).

## ISSUES IN EBP RESEARCH

Critiques of the application of EBP to eating disorders have noted the limitations based on constraints of randomized controlled trials (RCTs) and other research design restrictions. The relevance to actual practice has been questioned based on study selection decisions regarding sample population, interventions, salient factors, and outcome measures, and also, the failure to address multicultural counseling issues. Each of these issues is very important in the college context.

### Research Subject Selection

In order to comply with the research methodology, treatment populations used in an AN or BN research study have been artificially restricted and the resulting sample selection no longer represents the population that would present in university health services for eating disorders. The EDNOS clients routinely get excluded, as do the many co-morbid clients who present with other problems along with the eating disorder. Seligman (1995), among others, has criticized this aspect of RCTs because they select for only one diagnosis using a large number of exclusion criteria while, in actual practice settings, including college student psychotherapy, most clients have multiple problems, especially clients toward the more severe end of the symptom spectrum.

Westen, Novotny, and Thompson-Brenner (2004) identified several problematic methodological issues including the empirical and pragmatic limitations imposed by reliance on *DSM-IV* diagnosis and the problem of co-morbidity. Their review also noted the limits of generalizability due to the way that researchers versus clinicians assess for co-morbidity. They observe that researchers advertise for one disorder, while in actual practice, the initial client presentation may not remain as the primary diagnosis. Westen et al. estimate that from 1/3 to 1/2 of all those presenting for treatment might be excluded as subjects for any given study.

### Treatment Interventions and Other Factors

EBP studies have focused principally on the examination of type of therapeutic intervention. Specific treatments have been subject to testing and compared to purposely contrasting treatments, leading to the study of artificially rigid interventions. The appeal of manualized treatment is that therapists can adhere to a particular set of interventions that are allegedly more likely to lead to positive treatment outcomes. Westen et al. (2004) call for a change "from providing clinicians with step-by-step instructions for treating decontextualized symptoms or syndromes to offering them empirically supported theories of change that they can integrate into empirically informed treatments" (p. 658). They question why the CBT manual is limited to its current form and ask about adding affect regulation or addressing interpersonal problems components or changing the order or number of treatment sessions. Their point is that, at present, it is unlikely that any of these variables would be tested, even though they could be justified by theory for inclusion and could favor more efficacious choice of the treatment. They note that selecting what treatment to test is often "pre-scientific" in itself and thus can lead to scientifically invalid conclusions.

Conceptual frameworks regarding the etiology of eating disorders affect directions in devising treatment strategies. Nearly 20 years ago, Johnson and Connors (1987) described a biopsychosocial conceptualization of the etiology of bulimia, including bioenegetic, familial, and sociocultural factors. Such a biopsychosocial model seems to fit many of the students with eating disorders seeking our services. Striegel-Moore and Cachelin (2001) cited several theoretical models in their review of the etiology of eating disorders, all of which are multifactorial, albeit differing in emphasis placed on various risk factors (sociocultural, familial and interpersonal, personal vulnerability factors, and traumatic life events). They called for future research which considers various risk factors within an integrative framework that can assist in development of therapeutic interventions. Tylka and Subich (2004) conducted research on college women testing a multidimensional model that included sociocultural, personal and relational correlates ranging along a continuum of degree from no symptoms to clinical disorder. They found that the context of personal and relational variables may mediate or moderate the symptomology and suggest that treatment programs simultaneously address the different factors implicated in the multidimensional model.

In general, the EBP paradigm tests various treatments with the underlying assumption that the treatment intervention is the most salient factor. However, psychotherapy research has indicated that this is a mistaken notion, since the type of therapy used accounts for only a small portion of client outcome (Norcross, 2002). Other factors known to contribute include therapist and client characteristics and the qualities of the therapeutic relationship. Wampold (2001) observes that variability among providers delivering the same intervention is much greater than variability among types of interventions themselves, so it is grossly misleading to identify efficacious interventions while ignoring provider differences. Norcross (2001) reported extensive work to identify empirically supported therapy relationships and to determine ways to customize therapy to individual clients.

Similarly, Henry (1998) has regarded the narrowly construed EBP research as potentially damaging "pseudo-science" and calls for psychotherapy research designs that focus on central therapeutic processes. Albon and Marci (2004) note that the focus on evidence-based manualized treatments misses important information about what is efficacious about a given treatment and minimizes the importance of the clinical encounter within the therapeutic relationship. They also call for a shift in focus to a study of the change process rather than of the treatment type, and for bridging the gap between efficacy and effectiveness, studying therapy as it occurs in naturalistic settings, and attending more to patient contributions and to patient-therapist transactions. Given that many clients in university settings have a greater than average level of positive precursors for change (Hanna, 2004), therapeutic alliance and other common factors may be even more important.

### Outcomes

EBP outcomes, whether or not collected in college setting, tend to focus on symptom reduction rather than more global assessments of functioning. Even if looking at symptoms, it is unclear whether this means simply reduction or percentage of clients improved or recovered? Issues of statistical significance may be assumed to outweigh the more important goal of clinically significant change. For researchers looking at factors other than primary symptoms, decisions must be made about what other variables to include, how to assess them, and at what points to measure them. Outcome follow-up is often done upon completion of treatment, and the relapse issue, which is of great concern in eating disorders, is rarely addressed.

RCTs yield efficacy studies. Effectiveness studies are also needed to evaluate efficacy as applied to diverse settings by therapists with varying experience and expertise and with heterogeneous client groups. Before drawing conclusions about outcomes, clarity about how many subjects and how diverse a sample is needed is required in order to generalize the findings.

### Multicultural Concerns

In line with the above, EBP has been criticized for using homogeneous samples, and culture bound research methods, conceptualizations and treatment paradigms (Sue, 1999). Atkinson, Bui and Mori (2001) describe the EBP and the Multicultural Counseling movements as being on a collision course, both representing important developments in professional psychology that have rarely intersected. They list a number of issues that need to be addressed by EBP researchers from a multicultural perspective: subjects, symptom manifestations, acculturation, counselor multicultural competence, and relationship characteristics. The latter include variables such as linguistic similarity, racial/ethnic similarity, racial/ethnic identity development compatibility, and compatibility about causes and cures for psychological problems.

Similarly, Root (2001) states that more attention must be paid to cultural variations in the etiology, assessment and treatment of eating disorders. She underlines the need to test what has been considered "universal" on groups other than white Euro-American women, calling for studies on samples of Asian American, African American, Latina, and American Indians to determine whether ethnic group differences may influence eating disorder symptoms and suitability of treatments. Research reliance on patient samples inadvertently excluding ethnic minority groups may have created sampling bias that contributes to the perception that eating disorders mainly affect Euro-American populations (Striegel-Moore & Cachelin, 2001). Smolak and Striegel-Moore (2002) identify acculturation and discrimination specifically as issues faced by ethnic minorities that might impact the development of eating disorders. The relative lack of feminist and multicultural counseling formulations in devising EBP designs is especially troubling given the disparity in occurrence of eating disorders in women versus men and the acknowledged importance of cultural competence in evaluating usefulness of treatments (American Psychological Association, 2003; D.W. Sue & Sue, 2003).

## *GUIDING PRINCIPLES AND NEW MODELS FOR EVIDENCE-BASED PRACTICE*

Taking into account some of the limitations of EBP research, Wampold, Lichtenberg, and Waehler (2002) have provided some guiding principles regarding what they term empirically-supported interventions that are useful guidelines for campus-based future studies in this area: (1) Consider intervention level of specificity (e.g., moving from a most general level "psychotherapy" to more specific levels, such as "CBT," "CBT for BN," "CBT for BN with college women"; (2) Recognize the importance of other client variables (e.g., ethnicity, gender, attitudes and values, preferences for type of treatment); (3) Base conclusions on aggregate evidence, using meta-analysis methods; (4) Present evidence for absolute and relative efficacy (e.g., treatment better than nothing, treatment A better than B, and factors such as cost); (5) Make causal attributions for specific ingredients only if evidence is persuasive (e.g., legitimacy of the common factor models as opposed to the specific ingredient models); (6) Broaden assessment outcomes beyond symptom reduction to include general life functioning, perspective and cost/benefits from multiple perspectives (client, provider, third party payer); and (7) Assess outcomes at the local level and recognize freedom of choice. These seven principles have been endorsed by the Society of Counseling Psychology, American Psychological Association Division 17. They reflect the scientist-practitioner model where interventions follow from a scientific base and scientists conducting research are informed by those in practice. Counselors practicing in college mental health contexts would find these seven principles could serve as useful guides for investigations they might conduct.

## IMPLICATIONS AND CONCLUSIONS

Campus-based clinicians need to consider a number of issues in applying findings of EBP research to counseling center settings. Flexibility is required, since the faithful following of 15-20 session protocols for specific diagnoses may be difficult to implement. Specifically, the majority of college counseling centers use very brief therapy models (Archer & Cooper, 1998) and it is clear that the average number of counseling center sessions per client is far fewer than those called for in EBP protocols. Additionally, some students interrupt counseling due to breaks in the academic calendar and others may face session limit policies. Since many clients with eating disorders present with more than one problem, conceptualization and decisions about what to treat become important factors. Do you provide treatment for only one problem or do you address issues in a more integrated manner? Would the latter be sequential EBP protocols or a simultaneous incorporation of a variety of strategies based on EBP, clinical judgment and client characteristics? What if underlying issues, such as past childhood sexual abuse, are more significant in terms of treatment needs? Interdisciplinary interventions involving physicians, psychologists, and nutritionists are often the best practice with eating disorders (Hotelling, 2001), but such collaboration is rarely discussed in the EBP literature. Likewise, consideration of group counseling as a primary intervention or adjunct to individual therapy may be a preferred college counseling center practice (Archer & Cooper, 1998) yet is rarely mentioned.

Several other forces run counter to using current forms of EBP interventions in the college mental health context. Therapists working with college students typically use a multidimensional model of eating disorders that ranges along a continuum from a few symptoms to full-blown clinical disorder. Most students present as EDNOS, although this category is poorly defined and least studied (Striegel-Moore & Smolak, 2002). University and college counseling centers are committed to providing multiculturally sensitive counseling, which means recognition of group as well as individual and universal factors to inform assessment and treatment intervention, and therapist multicultural competence as it impacts treatment outcome. However, EBP research has not studied the role that these variables play. To address this shortcoming, the "Guidelines on Multicultural Education, Training, Research, Practice and Organizational Change for Psychologists" (American Psychological Association, 2003) must be incorporated into future EBP research paradigms. In light of these issues, few of the EBP interventions can be adopted "as is" at university and college counseling centers.

At this juncture, it would be premature to recommend exclusive use of only validated treatments and to withhold treatments for which there is not scientific evidence. The progress of scientific study of therapy in naturalistic settings is not sufficiently comprehensive to warrant such a position. Further, empirically unvalidated and empirically invalidated are not the same. It would be a wrong approach to dismiss the many interventions that have not been subjected to testing. Stein et al. (2001) cite several alternative treatments that need testing, such as feminist, stress-reduction, and Gestalt therapies. Garvin, Striegel-Moore, Kaplan, and Wonderlich (2002) call for further research on professionally designed self-help programs as potentially inexpensive and readily disseminated interventions and/or as adjuncts to other treatments, a strategy that could be readily employed in counseling centers should studies show support. Wampold et al. (2002) note that particular treatments deserve exclusive use if and only if the evidence of their superiority compared to other interventions is clear and persuasive.

Compelling evidence shows that studies of psychotherapy effectiveness must take into account client, counselor, and relationship characteristics (Atkinson et al., 2001; Norcross, 2002; Wampold, 2001). The

American Psychological Association president-elect (Levant, 2004) has set up a task force to produce a report recommending action with targeted messages for health care decision makers, payers, and psychologists. EBP is based on the Institute of Medicine (IOM) definition, with three equally valued components: (1) Best research evidence; (2) Clinical expertise; and (3) Patient values (Sackett, Strauss, Richardson, & Rosenberg, 2000). Evidence is broadly construed and therapist clinical judgment and therapeutic relationship are considered along with contextual and group factors. It is challenging to try to resolve the tension between conceptualizing the presenting problem in a way that addresses complexity and allows for flexibility in intervention while at the same time finds enough consistency in the treatment protocol to allow it to be evaluated and replicated. Meaningful evaluation measures are needed to go beyond symptom reduction and deal with broader as well as longer term outcomes. Such a multi-component perspective best fits college students with various eating disorder diagnoses.

Eating disorder studies reflect both advances in the EBP field and the limitations of studies to date. Nowhere is this contrast more evident than in the treatment of university students with ED diagnoses. As noted by Wampold et al. (2002), the current situation calls for a closer alliance between practitioners and scientists, so that each can inform the other and develop consensus on meaningful and valid interventions for complex presenting problems. University settings, with the proximity of academic departments to counseling service units, provide opportunities for such collaborations. As these application issues are resolved, EBP will be increasingly embraced in college settings, informing development of brief therapy treatment plans. Putting time and energy into this exploration makes very good sense in a setting where resources are scarce and accountability highly valued.

## REFERENCES

Albon, J.S., & Marci, C. (2004). Psychotherapy process: The missing link: Comment on Westen, Novotny, and Thompson-Brenner. *Psychological Bulletin, 130,* 664-668.

American Psychiatric Association. (1980). *Diagnostic and Statistical Manual of Mental Disorders* (3rd ed.). Washington, D.C.: Author.

American Psychiatric Association. (2000). *Diagnostic and Statistical Manual of Mental Disorders* (4th ed., text revision). Washington, D.C.: Author.

American Psychological Association. (2001). Empirically supported therapy relationships: Conclusions and recommendations of the Division 29 Task Force. *Psychotherapy: Theory, Research, Practice, Training, 38*, 495-497.

American Psychological Association. (2003). Guidelines on multicultural education, training, research, practice and organizational change for psychologists. *American Psychologist, 58*, 377-402.

Archer, J.A., Jr., & Cooper, S. (1998). *Counseling and mental health services on campus: A handbook of contemporary practices and challenges.* San Francisco: Jossey-Bass.

Atkinson, D.R., Bui, U., & Mori, S. (2001). Multiculturally sensitive empirically supported treatments–An oxymoron? In J. Ponterotto, J.M. Casas, L.A. Suzuki, & C.M. Alexander (Eds.). *Handbook of multicultural counseling* (2nd ed., pp. 542-574). Thousand Oaks, CA: Sage.

Barlow, D. H. (2000). Evidenced-based practice: A world view. *Clinical Psychology: Science and Practice, 7*, 241-242.

Chambless, D.L., & Hollon, S.D. (1998). Defining empirically supported therapies. *Journal of Consulting and Clinical Psychology, 64*, 497-504.

Garvin, V., Striegel-Moore, R.H., Kaplan, A., & Wonderlich, S.A. (2002). The potential of professionally based self-help interventions for the treatment of eating disorders. In R.H. Striegel-Moore, & L. Smolak (Eds.). *Eating disorders: Innovative directions in research and practice* (pp. 153-172). Washington, D.C.: American Psychological Association.

Hanna, F. J. (2004) *Therapy with difficult clients: Using the precursors model to awaken change.* Washington, DC: APA Press.

Henry, W.P. (1998). Science, politics and the politics of science: The use and misuse of empirically validated treatment research. *Psychotherapy Research, 8*, 126-140.

Herzog, B.B., & Delinsky, S.S. (2002). Classification of eating disorders. In R.H. Striegel-Moore, & L. Smolak (Eds.). *Eating disorders: Innovative directions in research and practice* (pp. 31-50). Washington, D.C.: American Psychological Association.

Hotelling, K. (2001). At last! Counseling Psychology and eating disorders. *The Counseling Psychologist, 29*, 733-742.

Johnson, C., & Connors, M.E. (1987). *The etiology and treatment of bulimia nervosa: A biopsychosocial perspective.* New York: Basic Books.

Levant, R. F. (2004, July-August). The empirically-validated treatment movement: A practitioner/educator perspective. In C. Goodheart & R.F. Levant (Co-chairs), *Best psychotherapy based on the integration of research evidence, clinical judgment, and patient values.* Symposium conducted at the meeting of the American Psychological Association, Honolulu, HI.

Norcross, J.C. (2001). Purposes, processes, and products of Task Force on Empirically Supported Therapy Relationships. *Psychotherapy: Theory, Research Practice, Training, 38*, 345-356.

Norcross, J. C. (Ed.). (2002). *Psychotherapy relationships that work: Therapist contributions and their responsiveness to patient needs.* New York: Oxford University Press.

Robin, A.L. (2003). Behavioral family systems therapy for adolescents with anorexia nervosa. In Kazdin, A.E., & Weisz, J.R. (Eds.). *Evidence-based psychotherapies for children and adolescents* (pp. 358-373). New York: Guilford Press.

Root, M.P.P. (2001). Future considerations in research on eating disorders. *The Counseling Psychologist, 29,* 754-762.

Sackett, D.L., Straus, S.E., Richardson, W.S., & Rosenberg, W. (2000). *Evidence based medicine: How to practice and teach EBM* (2nd ed). London: Churchill Livingstone.

Seligman, M.E.P. (1995). The effectiveness of psychotherapy. *American Psychologist, 50,* 965-974.

Smolak, L., & Murnen, S.K. (2002). Gender and eating problems. In R.H. Striegel-Moore, & L. Smolak (Eds.). *Eating disorders: Innovative directions in research and practice* (pp. 91-110). Washington, D.C.: American Psychological Association.

Smolak, L., & Striegel-Moore, R.H. (2002). Challenging the myth of the golden girl: Ethnicity and eating disorders. In R.H. Striegel-Moore, & L. Smolak (Eds.). *Eating disorders: Innovative directions in research and practice* (pp. 111-132). Washington, D.C.: American Psychological Association.

Stein, R.I., Saelens, B.E., Dounchis, J.Z., Lewczk, C.M., Swenson, A.K., & Wilfley, D.E. (2001). Treatment of eating disorders in women. *The Counseling Psychologist, 29,* 695-732.

Striegel-Moore, R.H., & Cachelin, F.M. (2001). Etiology of eating disorders in women. *The Counseling Psychologist, 29,* 695-732.

Striegel-Moore, R.H., & Smolak, L. (Eds.). (2002). *Eating disorders: Innovative directions in research and practice.* Washington, D.C.: American Psychological Association.

Sue, D. W. (2001). Multidimensional facets of cultural competence. *The Counseling Psychologist, 29,* 790-821.

Sue, D.W., & Sue, D. (2003). *Counseling the culturally diverse: Theory and practice* (4th ed.). New York, NY: John Wiley & Sons.

Sue, S. (1999). Science, ethnicity and bias: Where have we gone wrong? *American Psychologist, 54,* 1070-1077.

Tylka, T.L., & Subich, L.M. (2004). Examining a multidimensional model of eating disorder symptomology among college women. *Journal of Counseling Psychology, 51,* 314-328.

Wampold, B. E. (2001). *The great psychotherapy debate: Models, methods, and findings.* Mahwah, NJ: Lawrence Erlbaum.

Wampold, B. E., Lichtenberg, J. W., & Waehler, C. A. (2002). Principles of empirically-supported interventions in counseling psychology. *The Counseling Psychologist, 30,* 197-217.

Westen, D., Novotny, C.M., & Thompson-Brenner, H. (2004). The empirical status of empirically supported psychotherapies: Assumptions, findings, and reporting in controlled clinical studies. *Psychological Bulletin, 130,* 631-663.

Wilson, G.T. (1997). Cognitive behavioral treatment of bulimia nervosa. *The Clinical Psychologist, 50,* 10-12.

Wilson, G.T. (1999). Cognitive behavior therapy for eating disorders: Progress and problems. *Behaviour Research and Therapy, 34,* 197-212.

Wilson, G.T., & Fairburn, C.G. (2002). Treatments for eating disorders. In P.E. Nathan, & J.M. Gorman (Eds.). *A guide to treatments that work* (2nd ed., pp. 559-592). New York: Oxford University Press.

Wilson, G.T., Vitiusek, K.M., & Loeb, K.L. (2000). Stepped care treatment for eating disorders. *Journal of Consulting and Clinical Psychology, 68,* 451-459.

Wonderlich, S.A., Mitchell, J.E., Peterson, C.B., & Crow, S. (2002). Integrative cognitive therapy for bulimic behavior. In R.H. Striegel-Moore & L. Smolak (Eds.). *Eating disorders: Innovative directions in research and practice* (pp. 173-195). Washington, D.C.: American Psychological Association.

# Chapter 6.
# Supervising Counseling Center Trainees in the Era of Evidence-Based Practice

Jesse Owen
Karen W. Tao
Emil R. Rodolfa

**SUMMARY.** The role of Evidence-Based Practice (EBP) is increasing in importance for professional psychologists working in university counseling center contexts. As a result, providing training and supervision in EBP will be essential to the ability of college-based counselors to meet minimal standards of care. The focus of this paper is to provide a framework to foster critical thinking, to discuss the pedagogical assumptions of supervisors, and to provide suggestions for college counseling center supervisors to incorporate training in EBP into the expected competencies to be gained by interns and other trainees. *[Article copies available for a fee from The Haworth Document Delivery Service: 1-800-HAWORTH. E-mail address: <docdelivery@haworthpress.com> Website: <http://www.HaworthPress.com> © 2005 by The Haworth Press, Inc. All rights reserved.]*

Jesse Owen, MEd, is completing his internship at Counseling and Psychological Services, University of California, Davis, CA 95616 (E-mail: jjowen@ucdavis.edu).

Karen W. Tao, MA, is completing her internship at Counseling and Psychological Services, University of California, Davis, CA 95616 (E-mail: kwtao@ucdavis.edu).

Emil R. Rodolfa, PhD, is Director of Counseling and Psychological Services, University of California, Davis, CA 95616 (E-mail: errodolfa@ucdavis.edu).

[Haworth co-indexing entry note]: "Chapter 6. Supervising Counseling Center Trainees in the Era of Evidence-Based Practice" Owen, Jesse, Karen W. Tao, and Emil R. Rodolfa. Co-published simultaneously in *Journal of College Student Psychotherapy* (The Haworth Press, Inc.) Vol. 20, No. 1, 2005, pp. 67-77; and: *Evidence-Based Psychotherapy Practice in College Mental Health* (ed: Stewart E. Cooper) The Haworth Press, Inc., 2005, pp. 67-77. Single or multiple copies of this article are available for a fee from The Haworth Document Delivery Service [1-800-HAWORTH, 9:00 a.m. - 5:00 p.m. (EST). E-mail address: docdelivery@haworthpress.com].

**KEYWORDS.** Evidence-based practice, psychotherapy training and supervision, reflective judgment, cognitive complexity, counselor development

The era of evidenced-based practice (EBP) is a challenging time for psychology. Increasingly, clinicians, including those working on college campuses, are being held accountable for their assessment and treatment interventions. Bickman (1999) described two worlds of psychology in the 1990s, the academic world and the practice world. They were independent from one another, with academic freedom on one side or clinical freedom on the other, to do what they wanted. Clinical research was not viewed as helpful to clinicians because "real therapy" did not occur in the highly controlled and participant constrained environments where therapy process and outcome research occurred.

EBP, however, is where these two worlds meet. EBP allows the practicing psychologist working on campus a method to understand the factors that influence clinical or counseling practices. Cooper (2004) suggested that EBP takes into account factors influencing the creation of an effective therapeutic relationship, the determination of interventions most congruent with a client's characteristics, and the understanding of the theory and research literature relevant to a given client's specific problems and symptoms. EBP may find acceptance in many college counseling centers due to the centers' close proximity and relationship to academic psychology programs.

In this era of EBP, university mental health services supervisors need to help their supervisees develop the ability to make effective decisions regarding the most appropriate clinical treatment. Sound treatment strategies will be based on theory, evidence (broadly ranging from randomized controlled studies to case studies), and clinical expertise, taking into account client characteristics and relationship factors (Rodolfa, 2004). This chapter provides college counseling center supervisors a framework and suggestions for supervisees to incorporate evidenced-based thinking into their clinical practice. It is divided into three main segments. First "ways of knowing" and their relationship to counseling center psychologist development will be explored. Second, characteristics of the supervisory relationship will be discussed. Finally, suggestions for training programs, group seminars, and individual supervision that foster an enhanced understanding of EPB in college contexts will be described.

## WAYS OF KNOWING

Understanding the problems posed by college students as therapy clients is a central element for developing skills in EBP. Robinson and Halliday (1988) described many of the tasks counselors face as 'ill-structured.' In elaboration, King and Kitchener (1994) described 'ill-structured' problems as those having a level of uncertainty and ambiguity to their answers along with having the potential of multiple, equally valid solutions.

A pragmatic model of epistemology (ways of knowing) may assist supervisors to conceptualize how their supervisees think about ill-defined problems and make clinical judgments. The Reflective Judgment model (King & Kitchener, 1994) represents such a practical epistemological model. The Reflective Judgment model describes thinking as a function of how individuals view the certainty of knowledge, the acquisition of knowledge, and the process of making judgments (King & Kitchener, 1994) and is the most extensively researched theory of epistemology (Hofer & Pintrich, 1997; 2002). The Reflective Judgment model has seven stages of development: the first two stages are collectively called the Pre-reflective stages. Individuals at these stages of development rely heavily on authorities for answers, view knowledge as certain, and typically make decisions based on authorities' positions or personal experiences.

Individuals within the next three stages, aggregately labeled as the Quasi-reflective stages, experience knowledge as often uncertain, solutions are based on the idiosyncratic nature of the individual, and decisions are difficult to make, at times, due to the ambiguity of knowledge. Persons in the last two stages, collectively titled the Reflective stages, emphasize that the process of knowledge acquisition is through thoughtful and critical analysis of knowledge from experts and personal experience, acknowledging that though knowledge is uncertain, a probabilistic decision can be made with the information available.

This Reflective Judgment model appears consistent with the process of developing counseling skills. Typically beginning counselors, including those in college mental health settings, *seek* more structure and guidance (Stoltenberg, McNeil, & Delworth, 1998), whereas advanced trainees seek to analyze information more in depth and develop increasing autonomy. Research on the Reflective Judgment model and therapy is generally supportive. Debord (1993, cited in Wood, 1997) and Owen (2005) found that clinical and counseling trainees exhibited Quasi-Reflective thinking. In a related study, Skovholt and Ronnestad (1992) found that beginning counselors were more likely to rely on others for their knowledge about counseling whereas advanced counselors were more likely to rely on their experiences for knowledge. Collectively, these findings suggest that while beginning counselors may rely on "experts" for knowledge, they do not necessarily assume that the knowledge is absolute. More importantly, beginning counselors may not have the ability to analyze knowledge. This research highlights the importance of college counseling center supervisors assessing how their supervisees think about knowledge and how to appropriately challenge their assumptions to promote their supervisees' critical thinking and cognitive development.

## CHARACTERISTICS OF SUPERVISORY RELATIONSHIPS

One of the goals of supervision in university mental health settings is to help the supervisees think critically. However, prior to the actual work of supervision, a supervisory alliance must be developed to facilitate a supervisee's personal and professional development.

The following pertains to clinical supervision in general but holds for supervision conducted in the college counseling center context. Supervision is often experienced as a pedagogical adventure, where the supervisor, among many other tasks, must encourage the supervisees to articulate therapeutic intentionality (e.g., theory or research supporting particular interventions) and acknowledge their own limits of expertise and knowledge-base, while concomitantly managing interpersonal dynamics. The latter processes are highlighted, as it is the supervisor's level of self-awareness and ability to form a positive working alliance with their supervisees that will facilitate active participation in seeking knowledge in areas the supervisee experiences as unfamiliar or intimidating. Freire (1985) articulated that the process of knowing reality "presumes a dialectical situation: not strictly an 'I think,' but a "we think.' It is not the 'I think' that constitutes the 'we think,' but rather the 'we think' that makes it possible for me to think" (pp. 100-101). This quote illustrates the process within supervision in university mental health service units where moving away from the "I" to "we" opens the door to incorporation of new knowledge and acceptance of other ways of thinking and knowing.

While the bridge between science and practice has been demonstrated by scholars (Castonguay, Schut, & Constantino, 2000; Lampropoulos, Goldfried, Castonguay, Lambert, Stiles, & Nestoros, 2002) to be historically unwieldy, college counseling center supervisors are situated in a unique and critical position to reinforce how research and practice are inextricably linked. Nevertheless, to expect all supervisees to openly disclose uncertainties or doubts about their effectiveness in treatment and simultaneously provide evidence or rationale for their interventions with theory or research is unrealistic. Supervisors must recognize that the process of knowledge and skill integration will occur over time and be consistent with a supervisee's level of development (Castonguay, 2000). It is crucial to attend to *how* a supervisor engages with their supervisees and the roles they utilize to facilitate learning. The counseling center supervisors' attention to the balance between critique and validation, rhetoric and evidence-based discourse, and expert and novice dynamics are paramount to supervisee's training.

The supervisory relationship in university contexts may be viewed as bi-directional and reciprocal, imbued with communication that exhibits respect and openness for discussion and ranging in dialogical patterns reminiscent of teacher and student, colleague to colleague, therapist and client and expert and novice (Bernard & Goodyear, 2004). Initially, a supervisor may assume a teacher or expert role, but through an evolution and development of a strong working alliance, these roles may shift into peer, consultant or even silent observer. With more advanced supervisees, supervisors in college counseling centers are able to modify their roles according to the supervisee's developmental needs. Moreover, supervisors encourage supervisees to become initiators of their learning processes, including the right to provide constructive feedback to the supervisor and power to influence the direction of supervision. The level of self-efficacy and empowerment within supervision evolves through genuine and reciprocal engagement between supervisor and supervisees and by gradually recognizing the multiple roles they each play within the supervision process.

## TECHNIQUES TO PROMOTE EBP

In this section, we will provide supervisors working in college counseling center contexts a number of techniques to help promote thinking about EBP. We approach from a systemic perspective that includes the role of training programs, training seminars, and individual supervision. Accordingly, we believe that a systemic approach to EBP is vital to promote supervisor and supervisee development in university mental health settings.

## Training Programs

What role should campus-based training programs provide in the development of EBP? Recently, Falender and colleagues (2004) discussed the role of empirical evidence in supervision competencies. They stated " . . . science informed practice, as well as ethics of the profession, require professional practices to be based on science-derived knowledge; hence, knowledge of current research would be required" (p. 777). It is a daunting task for supervisors to keep abreast of the current research knowledge. However, college counseling center training programs can provide training, resources, and consultation to supervisors about current research. Because these training programs vary widely based on client population, treatment models, staff, and financial resources, we offer three broad recommendations: College counseling center training programs should:

1. Develop continuing education opportunities for supervisors to enhance their knowledge about current process and outcome research. This specific recommendation is made based on Sackett, Straus, Richardson, Rosenberg, and Haynes (2000) who commented that one of the barriers for supervisors to provide effective training in EBP is lack of knowledge about the current research.
2. Develop EBP protocols for their typical client populations. The format of the protocols could include supported treatments for particular disorders, cultural considerations, and general intervention process concerns. Over the years, supervisors and supervisees could revise and update these protocols, which will facilitate the transfer of knowledge when staff/trainees leave at the end of the training year.
3. Create an atmosphere of open discussion about the use of EBP in the delivery of services to their client population. This staff consultation could be facilitated by identifying experts in certain common disorders and problem domains as well as encouraging or even requiring staff consultation on a regular basis.

## Training Seminars

Training seminars delivered as an integral part of the counseling center's training program provide a useful structure for didactic instruction about EBP. We will describe an outline of a prototypical training seminar; however, it is important to be mindful of the developmental level of supervisees in the group. For instance, Owen (2005) noted that many graduate trainees are in the quasi-reflective stage of cognitive development. As such, they may struggle to accept that knowledge is uncertain, have difficulty differentiating from facts and interpretation, become challenged having to select among competing evidence-based research, accepting that knowledge may change at some future point when they will have to integrate changes into previous principles, and find it hard to construct their viewpoint and defend it based on evidence (King & Kitchener, 1994). Accordingly, the training seminar should provide a flexible structure of cognitive and emotional support and challenge.

Pre-instruction is important to set the expectations for such a seminar. The pre-instruction session should define ill-structured problems, EBP, and establish a decision making process. Hoge, Tondora, and Stuart (2003) outlined a decision making process for EBP. At first, university mental health supervisors should help their supervisees convert information into answerable questions and assist them to search for the best evidence to answer the question. Second, supervisors should assist their supervisees in appraising the evidence for its validity, impact, and clinical utility. Third, the supervisor can help the supervisee apply the evidence to the current clinical situation. Lastly, it is important for supervisors to evaluate the process and acknowledge potential barriers in the literature and in their personal expertise.

The instruction phase of the college counseling center EBP training seminar should be focused on both broad therapeutic concepts (e.g., common factors; see Wampold, 2002) and specific examples directly related to supervisees' cases (e.g., case presentations). Initially, the seminar should focus on how to find EBP information and how to evaluate the validity and the utility of the information found. After supervisees have an understanding of EBP, the seminar leaders can encourage or require the supervisees to present cases and relevant EBP information. The other seminar members should be encouraged to bring in alternative EBP information to help facilitate discussion. When cases are presented, seminar leaders may benefit from the following suggestions (King & Kitchener, 1994):

1. model evaluating arguments while detailing decision making process;
2. discuss alternatives and how they may be equally valid (or less so);
3. model holding and defending a point of view;

4. show flexibility with interpretations as new information is presented and model how to incorporate new information;
5. emphasize the difficulties inherent in working with ill-structured problems and support the supervisee's discomfort and struggle with the development of a cogent viewpoint.

It is important to emphasize that supervisees' participation in an EBP focused training seminar should help them develop the ability to make informed clinical judgments. Thus, the seminar leaders should facilitate trainees' cognitive development by guiding their thinking, not by telling them what to do.

## *Individual Supervision*

How often do campus-based supervisors ask "what does the research indicate when treating person X with Y disorder(s) in environment(s) Z?" The goal of incorporating EBP in supervision in university contexts is to enhance the supervisee's understanding of and critical thinking about mental health services. In order for professions to exist and grow, the members of the professions must not ignore current research. The question becomes how supervisors assist their supervisees to think about incorporating research into theory and in turn enhance their clinical experiences and expertise?

In facilitating this supervisory process, the supervisees' developmental stage should be taken into account. Castonguay (2000) noted that development of a therapeutic orientation is based on the process of assimilation and accommodation. As such, a supervisee will need a solid theoretical base to start. Accordingly, for beginning supervisees it is recommended that college counseling center supervisors emphasize one or two theoretical orientations and the supporting/contradictory evidence. This does not mean that EBP should be ignored for beginning supervisees. Quite the contrary, we suggest that establishing a solid argument for a therapeutic orientation should be based, in part, on empirical evidence. This process should increase the supervisee's depth of understanding of the theory and practice.

Initially during supervision, supervisors should discuss the nature of treatment and the role of EBP in treating college students. During this time, supervisors can provide tools for supervisees to find empirical based evidence (e.g., Bergin & Garfield's *Handbook of Psychotherapy and Behavioral Change 5th ed.*; Lambert, M. J. (Ed.), 2004). Further, supervisors will be able to guide the supervisee's understanding of the literature. Howard, McMillen, and Pollio (2003) suggested that studies should be analyzed based on efficacy ("Does the intervention work?"), effectiveness ("Does the treatment work under natural conditions?"), sensitivity ("Do service outcomes associated with an intervention differ across consumer subpopulations?"), and specification ("Does intervention X work for group Y when they are in setting Z?") (p. 245).

As supervision continues, supervisors can directly discuss how EBP applies to clinical cases. At first, the case discussion will most likely focus on clarifying the student's clinical issues and presenting concerns (i.e., assessment). After the problem(s) have been clarified, the supervisor should facilitate a discussion about conceptualization of the problem(s) and the therapeutic process utilizing counseling theory (e.g., Psychodynamic, Cultural considerations, etc.). This discussion will provide a foundation upon which to assimilate new information. Based on the developmental level of the supervisee, the sequence of supervision will vary. Building upon the base to view the client, alternative EBP interventions should be introduced to provide support and/or challenge established theoretical and clinical considerations. Gambrill (1997; 2004) noted that common errors in this decision making process include justifying views rather than critically evaluating them, overestimating accuracy of personal background information, disregarding conflicting evidence, and stereotyping.

The supervision process should help supervisees working in college contexts understand their clients and potential treatment options. After discussing possible intervention strategies, new information collected in subsequent sessions will continue to provide additional opportunities to incorporate EBP and revise initial hypotheses. Throughout supervision, the supervisor and supervisee must evaluate the utility of EBP and the supervisee's implementation of EBP assessment and intervention strategies. The supervisor and supervisee should examine not only the intervention process, but should also examine the supervisee's emotions regarding the process of therapy and supervision.

In summary, supervision in college counseling centers is a process where supervisors educate supervisees to think autonomously, flexibly, and critically, the basis of EBP.

# REFERENCES

Bernard, J., & Goodyear, R. (2004) *Fundamentals of clinical supervision 3rd edition.* Boston: Pearson.

Bickman, L. (1999). Practice makes perfect and other myths about mental health services. *American Psychologist, 54,* 965-978.

Carroll, M. (1996). *Counseling supervision: Theory, skills and practice.* London: Cassell.

Castonguay, L. G. (2000). A common factors approach to psychotherapy training. *Journal of Psychotherapy Integration, 10*(3), 263-282.

Cooper, S. (2004) Best evidenced based practices in the provision of college mental health counseling. *Presentation at the Association of University and College Counseling Center Directors Annual Conference, October 11, 2004.*

Debord, K. (1993). Promoting reflective judgment in counseling psychology graduate education. Unpublished Master's thesis, University of Missouri-Columbia.

Falender, C. A., Cornish, J. A. E., Goodyear, R., Hatcher, R., Kaslow, N. J., Leventhal, G., Shafranske, E., & Sigmon, S. T. (2004). Defining competencies in psychological supervision: A consensus statement. *Journal of Clinical Psychology, 60*(7), 771-785.

Freire, P. (1985) *Politics of Education: Culture, power and liberation.* New York: Bergin & Garvey.

Gambrill, E. (1997). *Social work practice: A critical thinker's guide (2nd ed.).* New York: Oxford.

Gambrill, E. (2004). Teaching clinical decision making: Applying research on problem solving and decision making. *Presentation at Educational Leadership Conference, Washington, D.C., September 11, 2004.*

Garb, H. N. (1998). *Studying the clinician: Judgment research and psychological assessment.* Washington D.C.: American Psychological Association.

Hofer, B. K., & Pintrich, P. R. (1997). The development of epistemological theories: Beliefs about knowledge and knowing and their relation to learning. *Review of Educational Research, 67,* 88-140.

Hofer, B. K., & Pintrich, P. R. (2002). Personal epistemology: The psychology of beliefs about knowledge and knowing. Mahwah, NJ: Lawrence Erlbaum Associates, Inc.

Hoge, M., Tondora, J., & Stuart, G. (2003). Training in evidence-based practice. *Psychiatric Clinics of North America, 26,* 851-865.

Howard, M. O., McMillen, C. J., & Pollio, D. E. (2000). Teaching evidence-based practice: Toward a new paradigm for social work education. *Research on Social Work Practice, 13*(2), 234-259.

King, P. M., & Kitchener, K. S. (1994). *Developing reflective judgment: Understanding and promoting intellectual growth and critical thinking in adolescents and adults.* San Francisco: Jossey-Bass.

Lambert, M. J. (2004). *Bergin and Garfield's handbook of psychotherapy and behavioral change (5th ed.).* New York: John Wiley & Sons, Inc.

Lampropoulos, G. K., Goldfried, M. R., Castonguay, L. G., Lambert, M. J., Stiles, W. B., & Nestoros, J. N. (2002). What kind of research can we realistically expect from the practitioner? *Journal of Clinical Psychology, 58*(10), 1241-1264.

Martinez, G.K., & Holloway, E.L. (1997). The supervision relationship in multicultural training. In D.B. Pope-Davis & H.L.K. Coleman (Eds.). *Multicultural counseling competencies: Assessment, education and training, and supervision. Multicultural aspects of counseling series. Vol. 7* (pp. 325-349). Thousand Oaks: CA, US: Sage.

Owen, J. J. (2005). Counselors' Reflective Judgment: An Examination of Clinical Judgment Approaches. Dissertation in progress. University of Denver.

Robinson, V. M. J., & Halliday, J. (1988). Relationship of counselor reasoning and data collection to problem-analysis quality. *British Journal of Guidance and Counselling, 16*(1), 290-295.

Rodolfa, E. (2004) Teaching evidence based practice at university counseling centers. *Presentation at the Association of University and College Counseling Center Directors Annual Conference. Lake Tahoe, Nevada, October 11, 2004.*

Sackett, D., Straus, S., Richardson, W., Rosenberg, W., & Haynes, R. (2000). *Evidence-based medicine: How to practice and teach EPM (2nd Ed).* New York: Churchill Livingstone.

Skovholt, T. M., & Ronnestad, M. H. (1992). Themes in therapist and counselor development. *Journal of Counseling & Development, 70,* 505-515.

Stoltenberg, C., McNeil, B. W., & Delworth, U. (1998). *IDM supervision: An integrated developmental model for supervising counselors and therapists.* San Francisco: Jossey-Bass.

Wampold, B.E. (2002). *The great psychotherapy debate: Models, methods, & findings.* Mahwah, NJ: Lawrence Erlbaum.

Wood, P. K. (1997). A secondary analysis of claims regarding the reflective judgment interview: Internal consistency, sequentiality and intra-individual differences in ill-structured problem solving. In J. Smart *(Ed.) Higher Education: Handbook of Theory and Research (vol. 11),* 245-314. New York: Agathon Press.

# Chapter 7.
# Evidence-Based Psychotherapy in College Mental Health: Common Concerns and Implications for Practice and Research

Stewart E. Cooper

**SUMMARY.** This synopsis chapter begins with a review of the main points each of the contributing authors made in their respective articles to this special publication on evidence-based practice in college counseling. A listing and explication of their common concerns about the applicability of EBPs for university mental health then follows. Finally, implications and suggestions for practice and research of evidence- based psychotherapy in college counseling center contexts are presented. *[Article copies available for a fee from The Haworth Document Delivery Service: 1-800-HAWORTH. E-mail address: <docdelivery@haworthpress. com> Website: <http://www. HaworthPress.com> © 2005 by The Haworth Press, Inc. All rights reserved.]*

**KEYWORDS.** Evidence-based practice, college mental health, college counseling centers

Stewart E. Cooper, PhD, ABPP, is Director of Counseling Services and Professor of Psychology at Valparaiso University, 826 La Porte Avenue, Valparaiso, IN 46383.
Address correspondence to: Stewart Cooper (E-mail: stewart.cooper@valpo.edu).

[Haworth co-indexing entry note]: "Chapter 7. Evidence-Based Psychotherapy in College Mental Health: Common Concerns and Implications for Practice and Research." Cooper, Stewart E. Co-published simultaneously in *Journal of College Student Psychotherapy* (The Haworth Press, Inc.) Vol. 20, No. 1, 2005, pp. 79-87; and: *Evidence-Based Psychotherapy Practice in College Mental Health* (ed: Stewart E. Cooper) The Haworth Press, Inc., 2005, pp. 79-87. Single or multiple copies of this article are available for a fee from The Haworth Document Delivery Service [1-800-HAWORTH, 9:00 a.m. - 5:00 p.m. (EST). E-mail address: docdelivery@haworthpress.com].

This special volume on evidence-based psychotherapy in college mental health has focused on four major clinical issues of significance in counseling with university students and has also addressed the important domain of training the next generation of practitioners. This summary chapter will discuss the main points each of the contributing authors made in their respective chapters and then will identify their common concerns about the applicability of EBPs to college counseling centers. Finally, recommendations for EBP informed university mental health practice and research will be given.

The chapter on alcohol related treatment by Ian T. Birky is an important contribution to the college counseling literature. Most articles in this field focus on prevention rather than counseling. Dr. Birky presents a summary of literature that some basis for EBP exists for the general population with differing interventions receiving some support. His sharing of specific studies conducted on this topic within university counseling centers show that insufficient evidence exists to imply inclusion or exclusion of any treatment but that a focus on building on strong therapeutic alliance had received the strongest support. His argument that most students who receive alcohol counseling are mandated and most do not have an abuse or dependency problem has major implications for clinical practice and for future investigations. Like the Eating Disorders chapter, Dr. Birky calls for a more conscientious selection of assessment and evaluation tools that assess areas germane to success in the college environment.

The chapter on depression by Carolyn L. Lee gives the reader a background on the nature of EBP research and specifically on the treatment of depression. She shares studies documenting the effectiveness of both cognitive-behavioral and interpersonal approaches in alleviating depression in the general adult clinical population. However, her chapter also discusses several significant discrepancies between the typical EBP research study and psychotherapy as it is conducted in college counseling centers. Due to these several discrepancies, Dr. Lee articulates several arguments against overly relying upon EBP as sole or even primary determination of intervention selection for college-based therapy.

The chapter on treatment of anxiety disorders by Thomas Baez similarly summarizes the EBP literature identifying successful approaches that have received support as reducing the various anxiety disorders. The investigations he presents in his chapter show, in general, that both behavioral and cognitive treatments work well with one or the other being somewhat superior depending on the specific type of anxiety disorder. As another parallel to the depression chapter, Dr. Baez reports that very few such studies have been conducted by counselors working in university mental health settings. His anxiety chapter includes a focus on the major issue of symptom co-morbidity and of the effects and importance of the college academic environment. At the end of his chapter, he urges practical research on anxiety reduction among college students by professionals working in this setting. He adds that such investigations should emphasize a focus on the therapeutic relationship and therapeutic process.

The chapter on eating disorders by Jaquelyn Liss Resnick presents definitions and evidence-based practice findings for its four main variants: Anorexia Nervosa, Bulimia, Eating Disorders Not Otherwise Specified (EDNOS), and Binge Eating Disorders. Her literature discloses that, by and large, relatively little about evidence-based practice has been found in the treatment of the general ED clinical population, and most of this is for Bulimia alone. Again, very few studies have focused on samples of these clients in the college counseling setting. The fact that most clients with ED receiving services at college counseling centers are EDNOS and that many have sub-clinical or mild levels of these syndromes seems particularly important for those working with this population.

Dr. Resnick's article makes a strong case for the difficulties of wholesale adapting of EBP to university settings. She covered several issues of concern including EBP research paradigms, populations studied, treatment interventions selected, and utilization of appropriate assessment indices and meaningful outcome measures. She also expresses that multicultural considerations have not been adequately incorporated. In sum, her chapter conveys that EBPs for EDs have very limited connection to current college counseling center psychotherapy practice. Most clients in this context have some co-morbid issues and almost all therapists use some form of integrative treatment.

Toward the end of the chapter, Dr. Resnick makes suggestions about current practice and research. In particular, she calls caution in over-reliance on EBP studies alone to make treatment selections and strongly advocates including in research both clinical expertise and patient values. She similarly argues that studying the therapeutic relationship and other factors common to all psychotherapy should receive priority in order for the field to advance. The use of meaningful, multi-component measures will be needed for such investigations. Dr. Resnick concludes her chapter stating that a closer alliance between practitioners and scientists is needed and would be mutually beneficial. Each group can inform the other and develop consensus on meaningful and valid interventions for complex presenting problems.

The chapter that focuses on incorporating EBP into college mental health training programs by Owen, Tao, and Rodolfa addresses the important issue of assisting practicum students and interns at varying levels of professional development to incorporate the current state of knowledge and uncertainty regarding EBPs into their work with college students. They advocate that supervisors and trainers use the "Reflective Judgment" model. Their chapter then goes on to describe issues of importance to clinical supervision relationship in general, and how that often morphs from assuming a teacher and expert role with lesser experienced trainees to a more collaborative peer, consultant, or even silent observer role with more developmentally advanced trainees. Without such a transition, training in incorporating EBPs is not likely to succeed.

The final part of their chapter discusses three suggestions for advancing discussion and engagement with EBPs in college counseling centers. Their first suggestion is that college counseling center training programs should develop opportunities for supervisors to enhance their knowledge about current EBP-related process and outcome research. Their second suggestion is that college counseling center training programs should develop EBP protocols for their typical client populations. The format of the protocols could include supported treatments for particular disorders, cultural considerations, and general intervention process concerns. Their third suggestion is that college counseling center training programs should create an atmosphere of open discussion about the use of EBP in the delivery of services to their client population. These authors strongly advocate use of a planned and organized intern training seminar.

## COMMON CONCERNS ABOUT APPLICABILITY OF EBP TO COLLEGE COUNSELING CENTER PRACTICE

All four chapters on EBPs and clinical syndromes listed common themes concerning the misapplication of findings from the EBP literature to work with college students receiving therapy in university mental health contexts. These common threads fall into five domains.

### Domain 1: Paucity of College Counseling Center EBP Investigations

For depression, anxiety, eating disorders, and alcohol use disorders, the vast majority of current EBP literature has been collected from clients in the general adult population receiving treatment in funded test sites. In each of these four areas, the respective authors' culling of the research databases and journals found a significant lack of college counseling center based EBP studies, which raises a significant concern about the generalizability of the existing EBP findings to the college context.

## Domain 2: Significant Difference Between Clinical Practice in College Counseling Centers versus Clinical Practice Employed in EBP Research Studies

In all four of the disorders chapters, the authors commented on the significant differences in psychotherapy as practiced in university mental health versus the standardized treatment protocols followed in EBP investigations. Most college counseling comprises only what could be viewed as very brief therapy, often only single session. In contrast, "brief therapy" in the EBP literature typically consists of 20 or more sessions. A second difference is the level of symptom severity. While a number of college students do present with severe symptoms, many have milder levels as compared to EBP study populations. For example, the largest category of eating disorders clients on campus would have a diagnosis of EDNOS, the least studied of all the EDs, and most students receiving counseling for alcohol issues would not meet the criteria for alcohol abuse or dependency. Yet, symptom co-morbidity is very common among college student clients if they have more severe problems in any given area, which such morbidity is screened out of the majority EBP study samples. Another significant difference between college mental health and EBP study practice is that most counselors working on campus have an eclectic or integrative approach whereas EBP protocols stress strict intervention adherence to a single approach. The effects of all the above differences call into question the applicability of EBP findings, certainly in the strict sense of following a rigid treatment regimen.

## Domain 3: Uniqueness of the University Context

This uniqueness plays out in two main ways. First, the ebbs and flows of the academic term strongly affect student stress levels and the way students view and work with their schedules. In EBP studies, the counseling follows a regimented schedule that, typically, is not interrupted.

Scheduling sessions in college counseling, though, is strongly influenced by the semester schedule. Sometimes this is because the likely stress levels are exacerbated (e.g., during mid-term exams) and often because of an academic break, the end of the term, transfer to another school, or graduation. The other unique aspect to counseling in college contexts is the nature of evaluation data that should be collected. EBP studies typically use well standardized (and typically expensive) general psychosocial functioning assessment instruments, which, typically, do not include items that are salient on campus such as better grades or attending classes, or retention. All authors advocated for use of items of particular relevance to the university environment and free or less expensive assessment options.

### Domain 4: Over-Focus on Studying Interventions

All authors commented on the over-focus of EBP research on specific interventions to treat particular disorders. The common view expressed was that in college mental health, research should emphasize "common factors" such as the therapeutic alliance as such common factors appear to be receiving support for their importance in psychotherapy generally and may be even more important in working with such a very brief therapy model. The authors also commented on the need to include assessment of client factors. Multi-campus research consortiums such as the Research Consortium of Counseling and Psychological Services (Counseling and Mental Health Center at The University of Texas in Austin), and Suffolk University among others (Counseling Center Village web page) (*http://ubcounseling.buffalo.edu/rn.html*) may offer the best chance for EBP research of this type.

### Domain 5: Ignoring Multicultural Factors

Most authors mentioned that the existing EBP literature fails to adequately address issues of culture. The typical EBP study uses a one size fits all approach, whereas facilitating and encouraging staff to conduct college counseling center based EBP research will be difficult, and current barriers will need to be overcome. Whenever possible, such studies should incorporate multicultural factors to allow analysis at that level and to evaluate facets that are differentially effective with one group over another.

## SUGGESTIONS FOR PRACTICE AND RESEARCH

Despite the above, pressures to further use EBPs within college counseling is likely to continue to grow in these next few years. Resnick predicts that "EBP will be increasingly embraced in college settings, informing development of brief therapy treatment plans. Putting time and energy into this exploration makes very good sense in a setting where resources are scarce and accountability highly valued." Yet, the very scarcity of resources greatly limits research. Methods to better incorporate these into practice and supervision will need to be developed and implemented. The chapter by Owen, Tao, and Rodolfa on training offers several practical ideas for achieving this.

For practitioners, campus-based or otherwise, the key challenge is how to engage in evidence-based practice when the evidence for the effectiveness of interventions comes from randomized stringently controlled trials using patient populations significantly different from the clinician's clients and using treatment manuals that appear simplified and overly rigid (Edwards, Dattilio, & Bromley, 2004). Messer (2004) advocates for clinicians to use a combination of theoretical formulation, empirically supported treatments, empirically supported therapy relationships, clinical experience, and clinical judgment.

For college counseling center therapists, the main implication seems to be the push to have a solid understanding of the EBP literature and what it does and does not signify regarding treatment, especially in the university environment. A focus on the currently emerging EBP literature on common factors may be useful and the work by Norcross and others within APA Division 29 seems to offer much promise. Their emerging synthesis would seem to indicate strongly that high quality studies of psychotherapy effectiveness should incorporate client, counselor and relationship characteristics (Atkinson et al., 2001; Norcross, 2002; Wampold, 2001). It could be that as most students have above average intelligence, such common factors have more of an effect on treatment outcome than do specific therapeutic interventions as these students have the cognitive flexibility to benefit from a range of suitable change strategies given a "good enough" counseling relationship.

For campus based researchers, a new paradigm is being developed by the American Psychological Association's "APA Presidential Initiative on Evidence-Based Practice (EBP) in Psychology" (Levant, 2005). The primary focus of this change is to enhance the importance of using multiple sources of research evidence plus clinical expertise plus patient values. The three components from the Institute of Medicine that define EBP are: (1) to consider a broader range of research evidence, (2) to explicate the application and appropriate role of clinical expertise in treatment decision making, and (3) to articulate a role for patient values in treatment decision making.

The seven guiding principles for EBP studies suggested by Wampold, Lichtenberg, and Waehler (2002), mentioned by several of the authors, would support the above. Both sets of suggestions reflect the scientist-practitioner integration where practitioners use interventions that follow from a scientific base and scientists conducting research are informed by those in practice. EBPs offer the opportunity for clinicians and researchers to come together in new ways that will enhance both and will better serve clients. McCabe states that EBPs offer the promise of reducing inappropriate practice and improving outcomes, but that progress will emerge only slowly from a coalescence of experimental data, clinical experience, and common sense. Incorporation of qualitative research methods, including case studies, which are more easily used by clinicians, is being advocated by many (e.g., Messer, 2004). Such integration of practice and science could be exciting to many who work in college counseling centers as it fits this culture well.

## REFERENCES

Atkinson, D.R., Bui, U., & Mori, S. (2001). Multiculturally sensitive empirically supported treatments–An oxymoron? In J. Ponterotto, J.M. Casas, L.A. Suzuki, & C.M. Alexander (Eds.). *Handbook of multicultural counseling* (2nd ed., pp. 542-574). Thousand Oaks, CA: Sage.

Baez, T. (2005). Evidenced-based practice for anxiety disorders in college mental health. *Journal of College Student Psychotherapy, 20*(1), 33-48.

Birky, I. (2005). Evidence-based and empirically supported college counseling center treatment of alcohol related issues. *Journal of College Student Psychotherapy, 20*(1), 7-21.

Edwards, D. J., Dattilio, F. M., & Bromley, D. B. (2004). Developing evidence-based practice: The role of case-based research. *Professional Psychology: Research and Practice, 35*, 589-597.

Lee, C. (2005). Evidenced-based treatment of depression in the college population. *Journal of College Student Psychotherapy, 20*(1), 23-31.

Levant, R. (2005, Feb.). Evidence-based practice in psychology. *Monitor on Psychology, 36*(2), 5.

Messer, S. B. (2004). Evidence-based practice: Beyond empirically supported treatments. *Professional Psychology: Research and Practice, 35*, 580-588.

Norcross, J. C. (Ed.). (2002). *Psychotherapy relationships that work: Therapist contributions and their responsiveness to patient needs.* New York: Oxford University Press.

Owen, J., Tao, K., & Rodolfa, E. (2005). Supervising Counseling Center Trainees in the Era of Evidence-Based Practice. *Journal of College Student Psychotherapy, 20*(1), 67-77.

Resnick. J. (2005). Evidence-based practice for treatment of eating disorders. *Journal of College Student Psychotherapy, 20*(1), 49-65.

Wampold, B. E. (2001). *The great psychotherapy debate: Models, methods, and findings.* Mahwah, NJ: Lawrence Erlbaum.

# Index

Academic performance, impact of
anxiety disorders on, 35,37,
42-43
Accountability, evidence-based
practice, 50
Agoraphobia, 36
Alcohol abuse, anxiety disorders
associated with, 37,42-43
Alcohol abuse treatment
co-morbidity issue in, 16
evidence-based, 7-21,80
attitudinal change techniques, 12
Bayesian approach to, 9
behavioral therapy, 10
brief therapy, 11-12,13,17-18
cognitive-behavioral coping
skills training, 10
cognitive therapy, 10
cue exposure therapy, 10
demographic factors in, 16-17
*Diagnostic and Statistical
Manual of Mental
Disorders-IV* and, 15,16
in general *versus* college
populations, 82-83
grants-based funding for, 8
limitations of, 12,13-14
meta-analysis of, 9,10
models for, 17-18
motivational enhancement
therapy, 10
outcome measures in, 13
overview of, 9
personalized educational
strategies, 11-12
primary prevention-based
analysis of, 11
recommended approach in,
14-17

referrals to, 15-16
reinforcement-based
interventions, 10
single-session interventions, 11,
12
skills-based approaches in, 12
social norm strategies, 11-12
social skills training therapy, 10
supportive-expressive therapy,
10
12-step facilitation therapy, 10
urge coping skills training, 10
therapeutic relationship in, 39-40
Amenorrhea, anorexia nervosa-related,
52
American College Health Association,
24
American Psychiatric Association,
practice guidelines of, 2
American Psychological Association
"APA Presidential Initiative on
Evidence-Based Practice"
(EBP) in Psychology," 85-86
Clinical Psychology Division,
practice guidelines, 2
criteria for treatment guidelines,
28-29
Division 17, 60
Special Task Group, 17
Division 29, 85
Division of Counseling Psychology,
3-4
"Guidelines on Multicultural
Education, Training,
Research, Practice and
Organizational Change for
Psychologists," 61
Anorexia nervosa, 50-51
evidence-based therapy for

cognitive-behavioral therapy, 51
family therapy, 51
research subject selection in, 56
treatment outcomes in, 51
subtypes of, 51
symptoms of, 51
Antidepressant therapy, for bulimia
nervosa, 54
Anxiety/anxiety disorders, 33-48
bulimia nervosa-related, 54
categories of, 34
comorbidities
depression, 35
posttraumatic stress disorder, 37
substance abuse, 35
suicidal thoughts, 35
evidence-based psychotherapy for,
35-48
for chronic anxiety, 42-44
in college populations,
37-39,40-46
in the general population, 35-37
in general *versus* college
populations, 82-83
research guidelines for, 40-42
therapeutic relationship in,
39-40
impact on academic performance,
35,37,42-43
incidence of, 34
public speaking-related, 37-38,39
relaxation therapy for, 43,44
risk factors for, 34
Attitudinal change techniques, for
alcohol abuse treatment, 12


Beck Depression Inventory (BDI), 41
Behavioral therapy, for alcohol abuse,
10
Behavioral weight loss (BWL), 55
Bibliotherapy, stress inoculation, 38,39
Binge eating
binge eating disorder-related, 55
bulimia nervosa-related, 52,53,54

Binge eating disorder, 50-51,54,55
Biopsychosocial model, of bulimia
nervosa, 57
Brief Symptom Inventory (BSI), 43
Brief therapy, 4,85
for alcohol abuse, 11-12,13,17-18
for depression, 26-28
*versus* standardized treatment
protocols, 83
Bulimia nervosa, 50-51,52-54
antidepressant therapy for, 54
anxiety associated with, 54
binge eating associated with,
52,53,54
biopsychosocial model of, 57
clinical features of, 52
depression associated with, 54
evidence-based psychotherapy for
cognitive-behavioral therapy,
52-53,54
integrative cognitive therapy,
53-54
interpersonal psychotherapy, 53
research subject selection and,
56
research subject selection in, 56
stepped-care therapy, 54


Case studies, 5
*Chronicle of Higher Education,* 2-3
Clinical psychology trials, of
depression treatment,
24-25,26-27
Cognitive-behavioral coping skills
training, as alcohol abuse
treatment, 10
Cognitive-behavioral therapy
for anorexia nervosa, 51
for anxiety disorders, 35
for binge eating disorder, 55
for bulimia nervosa, 52-53,54
for depression, 24,25,28
manualized, for public
speaking-related anxiety, 38

for panic disorder
  effect of therapist's efficacy on,
    39
  in the general population, 36-37
  for phobias, 35-36
Cognitive restructuring, as generalized
    anxiety disorder treatment,
    38,39
Cognitive therapy
  for alcohol abuse, 10
  for anxiety disorders, 35
College counseling centers,
    evidence-based practice in,
    obstacles to, 4-5
Counseling Center Care Bill, 44
Counseling Center Village web page,
    44,84
Counselors, college-based, training and
    supervision of, 67-77
  evidence-based
    psychotherapy-promoting
    techniques in, 71-75
  individual supervision in, 74-75
  reflective judgment model for,
    69-70,82
  supervisory relationship in, 70-71
  training programs in, 72
  training seminars in, 72-74
  "ways of knowing" approach in,
    68,69-70
Critical Incidents Stress Debriefing,
    2-3
Cue exposure therapy, for alcohol
    abuse, 10

"Debriefing Debate, The" (Glenn), 2-3
Depression
  anxiety disorders-related, 35,42-43
  bulimia nervosa-related, 54
  definition of, 24-25
  evidence-based psychotherapy for,
    23-31
    acceptability to the patient
    criteria for, 28,29

as brief therapy, 26-28
clinical judgment and expertise
  criteria for, 28-29
clinical trials of, 24-25,26-27
cognitive-behavioral therapy,
  24,25,28
empirical research criteria in, 28
in general *versus* college
  populations, 82-83
interpersonal therapy,
  24,25,28,29
number of sessions in, 27-28
risk factors for, 26
symptoms of, 24-25
*Diagnostic and Statistical Manual of
  Mental Disorders-III-*(DSM-III),
  24-25,51
*Diagnostic and Statistical Manual of
  Mental Disorders-IV*
  (DSM-IV), 15,16
*Diagnostic and Statistical Manual of
  Mental Disorders-IV-TR*
  (DSM-IV-TR), 50-51

Eating disorder not otherwise specified
  (EDNOS), 50-51,55,56,83
Eating disorders
  anorexia nervosa, 56
    cognitive-behavioral therapy for,
      51
    family therapy for, 51
    subtypes of, 51
    symptoms of, 51
    treatment outcomes for, 51
  binge eating disorder, 50-51,54,55
  bulimia nervosa, 52-54
    antidepressant therapy for, 54
    anxiety associated with, 54
    binge eating associated with,
      52,53,54
    biopsychosocial model of, 57
    clinical features of, 52
    cognitive-behavioral therapy for,
      52-53,54

depression associated with, 54
evidence-based therapy for, 56
integrative cognitive therapy for,
    53-54
interpersonal psychotherapy
    (IPT) for, 53
stepped-care therapy for, 54
definitions of, 50-51
eating disorder not otherwise
    specified (EDNOS), 50-51,55,
    56,83
etiology of, 57
evidence-based psychotherapy for,
    49-65,81
    in general *versus* college
        populations, 82-83
    issues in, 55-59
    limitations to, 55-56
    manual-based, 56-57
    meta-analysis in, 60
    multicultural issues in, 58-59,61
    outcomes in, 58,60
    principles and new models for,
        59-60
    randomized controlled trials in,
        55-56,58
    therapeutic relationship in,
        57-58
gender differences in, 50-59
prevalence of, 51
Eclectic approach, of college mental
    health counselors, 83
Empirically-based treatment (EBT),
    2,50
Empirically-supported interventions
    (ESI), 2,50
Empirically-supported relationships
    (ESR), 50
Empirically-validated treatment
    (EVT), 2,50
Epistemology, reflective judgment
    model for, 69-70,82
Ethnic minority groups, eating disorder
    evidence-based therapy with,
    59

Evidence-based practice (EBP), 2
    definition of, 86
Evidence-based psychotherapy, 7-21
    accountability in, 50
    for alcohol abuse, 7-21,80
        Bayesian approach to, 9
        behavioral therapy, 10
        cognitive-behavioral coping
            skills training, 10
        cognitive therapy, 10
        cue exposure therapy, 10
        *Diagnostic and Statistical
            Manual of Mental
            Disorders-IV* and, 15,16
        limitations of, 12,13-14
        meta-analysis of, 9,10
        models for, 17-18
        motivational enhancement
            therapy, 10
        outcome measures in, 13
        overview of, 9
        personalized educational
            strategies, 11-12
        primary prevention-based
            analysis of, 11
        recommended approach in,
            14-17
        referrals to, 15-16
        reinforcement-based
            interventions, 10
        single-session interventions, 11,
            12
        skills-based approaches in, 12
        social norm strategies, 11-12
        social skills training therapy, 10
        supportive-expressive therapy, 10
        12-step facilitation therapy, 10
        urge coping skills training, 10
    for anxiety disorders, 80-81
    attitudinal change techniques, 12
    brief therapy, 4,85
        for alcohol abuse, 11-12,13,17-18
        for depression, 26-28
        *versus* standardized treatment
            protocols, 83

common concerns about, 82-85
lack of inclusion of multicultural
factors, 84
lack of research about, 82-83
uniqueness of the university
setting, 83-84
demographic factors in, 16-17
for depression, 26-28,31-32,80
acceptability to the patient
criteria for, 28,29
clinical judgment and expertise
criteria for, 28-29
cognitive-behavioral therapy,
24,25,28
empirical research criteria for,
28
in general *versus* college
populations, 82-83
interpersonal therapy,
24,25,28,29
number of sessions in, 27-28
*Diagnostic and Statistical Manual
of Mental Disorders-IV* and,
15,16
for eating disorders, 49-65,81-82
in general *versus* college
populations, 82-83
issues in, 55-59
limitations to, 55-56
manual-based, 56-57
meta-analysis in, 60
multicultural issues in, 58-59,61
in general *versus* college
populations, 82-83
goals of, 50
grants-based funding for, 8
misuse of, 50
multicultural factors in, 84
practice and research
recommendations regarding,
85-86
session scheduling in, 83-84
Evidence-based psychotherapy, in
college mental health, 1-6

Evidence-informed interventions (EII),
50
Evidence-informed practice (EIP), 2
Exercise, excessive, as weight control
method, 52
Exposure-based therapy, for social
anxiety/phobia, 35,36
Eye-movement desensitization and
reprocessing (EMDR)
as posttraumatic stress disorder
treatment, 35,36
as public speaking-related anxiety
treatment, 37-38

Family therapy, for anorexia nervosa,
51
Fasting, as weight control method, 52
Fund for the Improvement of Post
Secondary Education
(FIPSE), 8

"Garrett Lee Smith Memorial Act," 44
Generalized anxiety disorder
evidence-based psychotherapy for
cognitive restructuring therapy,
38,39
stress inoculation therapy, 38
incidence of, 34
"Guidelines on Multicultural
Education, Training,
Research, Practice and
Organizational Change for
Psychologists" (American
Psychological Association),
61

*Handbook of Psychotherapy* (Bergin
and Garfield), 74-75
Health Insurance Portability and
Accountability Act (HIPPA),
45

Institute of Medicine, evidence-based
     practice definition of, 86
Institutional review boards (IRBs),
     41,45
Integrative cognitive therapy, for
     bulimia nervosa, 53-54
Internet-based treatment, of
     posttraumatic stress disorder,
     38
Interpersonal psychotherapy (IPT)
     for binge eating disorder, 55
     for bulimia nervosa, 53
     for depression, 24,25,28,29
In vivo exposure therapy
     for panic disorder, 35,36
     for phobias, 35-36
In vivo psychodrama-based
     desensitization (IVPBD), 38

Journaling, 43

Kansas State University, 24

Laxative abuse, 52

Managed care, 50
Medical model, 50
Mexican-American college students,
     38,39
Motivational enhancement therapy, for
     alcohol abuse, 10
Multicultural counseling movement,
     58-59
Multicultural factors, in
     evidence-based
     psychotherapy, 84
     for eating disorders, 58-59,61

National Institute of Mental Health,
     Treatment of Depression

Collaborative Research Project,
     27
"Nightmare Scenarios" (Glenn), 2


Obesity, as medical disorder, 51
Obsessive-compulsive disorder
     evidence-based psychotherapy for,
     35,36
     incidence of, 34
OCD. *See* Obsessive-compulsive
     disorder
Outcome Questionnaire (OQ-45), 43


Panic disorder
     evidence-based psychotherapy for
          cognitive-behavioral therapy,
          36-37,39
          effect of therapist's efficacy on,
          39
          in the general population,
          35,36-37
     incidence of, 34
Personalized educational strategies, in
     alcohol abuse treatment,
     11-12
Phobias, specific
     evidence-based therapy for, 35-36
     incidence of, 34
Posttraumatic stress disorder
     anxiety disorders-related, 37
     evidence-based psychotherapy for,
          in the general population,
          35,36
     incidence of, 34
     Internet-based treatment of, 38
Practice, relationship with research,
     70-71
*Professional Psychology: Research
     and Practice,* 3
Public speaking, as anxiety cause,
     37-38,39
Purging, bulimia nervosa-related, 52,
     53,54

Quality Assurance Project, 36

Randomized trials, 85
  in eating disorders treatment,
    55-56,58
Reinforcement-based interventions, for
    alcohol abuse, 10
Relaxation therapy
  for anxiety disorders, 35,43,44
  for phobias, 35-36
Research, relationship with practice,
    70-71
Research Consortium of Counseling
    and Psychological Services in
    Higher Education, 27,44,84

"Sandplay, Therapy, and Yoga"
    (Glenn), 2
September 11, 2001, 37
Session scheduling, in evidence-based
    psychotherapy, 83-84
Single-subject designs, 5
Skills-based approaches, in alcohol
    abuse treatment, 12
Social anxiety/phobias, evidence-based
    psychotherapy for, 35,36
Social norm strategies, for alcohol
    abuse treatment, 11-12
Social skills training
  as alcohol abuse treatment
  as social anxiety/phobia treatment,
    35,36
Society of Counseling Psychology, 60
Spiders, fear of, 38,39
Stepped-care therapy, 55
  for bulimia nervosa, 54
Stress inoculation bibliotherapy, 38,39
Stress inoculation therapy, for
    generalized anxiety disorder,
    38
Substance abuse. *See also* Alcohol
    abuse; Alcohol abuse
    treatment

anxiety disorders-related, 35
Suffolk University, 44,84
Suicidality, anxiety disorders-related,
    35,43
Supportive-expressive therapy, for
    alcohol abuse, 10
Symptom severity, 83
Systematic desensitization
  as phobia treatment, 35-36
  as social anxiety/phobia treatment,
    35,36

Therapeutic relationship, in evidence-
    based psychotherapy, 81,85
  in alcohol abuse treatment, 39-40
  in anxiety disorders treatment,
    39-40
  in eating disorders treatment, 57-58
  effect on therapeutic outcome, 3
  Working Alliance Inventory (WAI)
    assessment of, 41-42
Therapists, efficacy of, 39
Training and supervision, of
    college-based counselors,
    67-77
  evidence-based therapy-promoting
    techniques in, 71-75
  individual supervision in, 74-75
  reflective judgment model for,
    69-70,82
  supervisory relationship in, 70-71
  training programs in, 72
  training seminars in, 72-74
  "ways of knowing" approach in,
    68,69-70
Treatment of Depression Collaborative
    Research Project, 27
12-step facilitation therapy, for alcohol
    abuse, 10

United States Department of Education,
    8

University of Texas, Austin, Research
        Consortium of Counseling
        and Psychological Services in
        Higher Education, 44,84
Urge coping skills training, as alcohol
        abuse treatment, 10


Working Alliance Inventory (WAI),
        41-42

# BOOK ORDER FORM!

Order a copy of this book with this form or online at:
http://www.HaworthPress.com/store/product.asp?sku=5714

## Evidence-Based Psychotherapy Practice in College Mental Health

___ in softbound at $19.95 ISBN-13: 978-0-7890-3069-6 / ISBN-10: 0-7890-3069-1.
___ in hardbound at $29.95 ISBN-13: 978-0-7890-3068-9 / ISBN-10: 0-7890-3068-3.

COST OF BOOKS _____

POSTAGE & HANDLING _____
US: $4.00 for first book & $1.50
for each additional book
Outside US: $5.00 for first book
& $2.00 for each additional book.

SUBTOTAL _____

In Canada: add 7% GST. _____

STATE TAX _____
CA, IL, IN, MN, NJ, NY, OH, PA & SD residents
please add appropriate local sales tax.

FINAL TOTAL _____
If paying in Canadian funds, convert
using the current exchange rate,
UNESCO coupons welcome.

❏ BILL ME LATER:
Bill-me option is good on US/Canada/
Mexico orders only; not good to jobbers,
wholesalers, or subscription agencies.

❏ Signature _____

❏ Payment Enclosed: $ _____

❏ PLEASE CHARGE TO MY CREDIT CARD:
❏ Visa ❏ MasterCard ❏ AmEx ❏ Discover
❏ Diner's Club ❏ Eurocard ❏ JCB

Account # _____

Exp Date _____

Signature _____
*(Prices in US dollars and subject to change without notice.)*

### PLEASE PRINT ALL INFORMATION OR ATTACH YOUR BUSINESS CARD

| | |
|---|---|
| Name | |
| Address | |
| City | State/Province | Zip/Postal Code |
| Country | |
| Tel | Fax |
| E-Mail | |

May we use your e-mail address for confirmations and other types of information? ❏ Yes ❏ No We appreciate receiving
your e-mail address. Haworth would like to e-mail special discount offers to you, as a preferred customer.
**We will never share, rent, or exchange your e-mail address.** We regard such actions as an invasion of your privacy.

Order from your **local bookstore** or directly from
**The Haworth Press, Inc.** 10 Alice Street, Binghamton, New York 13904-1580 • USA
Call our toll-free number (1-800-429-6784) / Outside US/Canada: (607) 722-5857
Fax: 1-800-895-0582 / Outside US/Canada: (607) 771-0012
E-mail your order to us: orders@HaworthPress.com

**For orders outside US and Canada,** you may wish to order through your local
sales representative, distributor, or bookseller.
For information, see http://HaworthPress.com/distributors

*(Discounts are available for individual orders in US and Canada only, not booksellers/distributors.)*

**Please photocopy this form for your personal use.**
www.HaworthPress.com

BOF05